SKAB

Skin and Bones with a Few Ounces of Courage

Trevor Skrocki

Preface

On the road to the two-week program in Tewksbury, MA after my second DUI conviction, I was in the vehicle with my parents for attempt number two in admittance. Only this time, I knew I could actually be accepted into the program. I had been clean and sober for two weeks. During the ride, I wanted to get something to read for my stay and came across a book entitled "Moments of Clarity," by Christopher Kennedy Lawford. Unfortunately, I wasn't able to track down the book in time and was forced to manage my stay without it. However, I still made my way through the program with a better head on my shoulders, in an attempt for a real shot at recovery.

From day one, well pretty much since I returned from Tewksbury, I have let my voice of recovery be heard by the public. I wanted to let everyone know that I was "clean and sober" and in fact attempting a journey into long-term recovery. I felt that it was my duty to let people know that I wanted this lifestyle change. If I made sure that I got my point across, I could quite possibly get the necessary support from friends and family. I was amazed that so many people actually *cared* that I was putting an effort into getting well. The constant support of others, not only from my family and friends, but from friends of friends as well, has shown me that there is a greater support, a greater kind of grace, than I originally thought. There is actually a whole other side of support, from anybody and everybody, as I recently put "SKAB" into plain view for the outside world to see.

After reading "Moments of Clarity," I became more interested and involved in telling my story. I was always open and honest throughout the programs I went through during my initiation into recovery and I felt that I had a greater empowerment after reading the book. These people who were just telling their stories and letting their inner demons out were amazing. It takes courage to do that, and that's exactly what I was really going for. I wanted those "Few Ounces of Courage." I wanted to lay everything out on the table and be freed from those demons. The book made me realize my "Moment of Clarity," and inspired me to write "SKAB." I am not only thankful, but also grateful, it did so.

I want to thank my family, especially my mother Dianne, father Steve, and brother Ryan, for their constant support throughout my journey thus far. Without them, I don't know where I'd be right now. I want to thank all of my friends throughout this journey as well. God has blessed me with amazing friends, and it would take an enormous amount of time to name them all. They all have been supplying the fuel for the support I desperately need and have always been in my corner. I want to thank the Sookeys for everything they have done for me in my life as well. I never thought I'd have a second family growing up in this world.

This book is devoted to all those who are out there struggling with drugs and/or alcohol. It saddens my heart to see anybody go through the pain that drug addiction and alcoholism can present. There is help out there. There is hope out there. You only have to *be willing* to fight this disease. If I can do it, you can do it. Don't be afraid or ashamed of this disease by any means. Although it seems like a scary thing, especially to ask for help when you don't think you need it or even want it, remember me when I say this: "I am NOT a statistic, because I found my 'Moment of Clarity.'" I hope those of you out there struggling with this cruel disease can find yours. And I hope "SKAB" can help guide you in the right direction.

Part I: It's a Bumpy Road

My name is Trevor Skrocki, and I'm a recovering drug addict and alcoholic. I still have an uneasiness with these "labels," as coming to grips with them is a bit intimidating nonetheless. However, in reality they don't change who I am as a person. It was not my intention to be a drug addict or an alcoholic. Addiction is a disease for which there is no known cure; however, this growing notion of hope, otherwise known as recovery, is the best known solution. I have grown to accept these labels with prior knowledge and a recent understanding as you will hear in my story. I have been to AA before, but have not attended regularly or consistently. I have chosen to take my own route of Recovery, which I also like to refer to as "My Journey." Let's also remember that recovery is a journey, not a destination. I try to keep it simple, although it's not always easy, and I am a strong believer in taking my recovery *one day at a time*. This journey is a never-ending battle that needs constant guidance and has absolutely no room for failure. I'm working on not becoming complacent. I hope to help, reach out, and inspire others with my story as it helps me through my own recovery. This is my story.

I was born on March 16, 1986 and grew up in a small town of Adams, Massachusetts, where I have resided my entire life. I come from a caring family consisting of a loving mother and father and an older brother. I guess you could say my life was looking promising as a young child, as I excelled in school, was involved in competitive sports, and had many friends.

As a child I became involved in youth sports leagues in my hometown. I played basketball, baseball, and soccer. Throughout my youth I also participated in travel and all-star teams for all three sports. I won multiple free-throw and three-point competitions in basketball. I was evolving into a great shooter, and continued to progress as an athlete as the years went on. I was on a youth travel basketball team that won multiple basketball tournaments throughout Berkshire County. I was considered one of the best three-point shooters in the county as well. I won a Little League title my first year playing baseball. I began pitching my second year. Starting in my first game, I struck out ten batters and was the winning pitcher. I also played short-stop, where I excelled. I wasn't the best hitter, but was consistently getting on base. I also won a title during my Babe Ruth career, which was the next stage after Little League. I mainly played third base, because I had a strong arm. I played on travel soccer teams and ended up being a superb goalie. In my youth I was a goal scorer, three or four goals a game at times. As I grew taller into the middle school years, my coaches experimented with me as a goalie and I adjusted to be a good fit, shutting out opponents. I never pursued baseball or soccer into my high school years. Basketball was my love and I was committed to becoming a great player.

My life began to change at a young age, however, as I perceived myself as the skinny kid. I lost a great deal of self-esteem as I noticed a deformity in my chest. I would get out of the shower and see a sunken-in or caved-in chest, revealing my rib cage, which was grotesque through my eyes. I knew there was something wrong with me, but I always put it on the back burner and went on my way. I always felt like the odd kid and never wanted to take my shirt off. I remember when I did take my shirt off in public places, such as the beach, I always tried to cover my chest with my arm, pretending to itch my left shoulder with my right hand. Other times, when I was getting a picture taken of me with my shirt off, I would reveal my chest. I wanted to see firsthand how I looked from the outside looking in. Not being comfortable in my own skin was always an uneasy feeling. At age 14 I had a routine check-up with my doctor and he took a look at my chest. He referred me to a doctor who did surgical procedures in order to fix my problem. The deformity of my chest was called pectus excavatum. It's the most common congenital deformity of the anterior wall of the chest, in which several ribs and the sternum grow abnormally. I later read in one of the pamphlets that this disease occurs in 1 in 1,000 people. The doctor said this was one of the worst cases he had ever seen. So severe that my rib cage could crush my heart and kill me. Being a freshman in high school, this was a scary time in my life, and there was no doubt in my mind that surgery had to be done.

The procedure was done towards the end of my freshman basketball season at Hoosac Valley High School. When I awoke from surgery at Baystate Medical Center, I now had a metal rod implanted under my rib cage, which would have to stay in my body for two years. The pain was nothing I had ever felt before. Even your rather "tough guy" would have trouble dealing with the kind of pain I was in. I have always used the analogy of an elephant sitting on top of one's chest. I felt unbearable pain at times. In order to get out of bed in the morning I had to dangle my legs onto the floor and push my arms off the bed to sit my body upright. I really couldn't do much of anything for quite some time. I had to do all of my schoolwork at home. When I finally was able to go back to school I wasn't allowed in the hallways with all of the students, because I had to avoid people accidentally bumping into me. I was cautious. All physical activities were out of the question, but eventually my body began to heal and I was able to do some active things.

I wanted to point out this point of my life because at the time I had no idea what a painkiller was. I think my parents gave me a couple when I got home from the hospital, but I never took any more after that. I got through the recovery phase of surgery with no pain medication, which is quite the feat in itself. Being 14 years old, having such a serious and painful surgery of that magnitude, and getting by without even thinking about a pain killer was amazing. I really had no idea of that at the time, but now I do.

The first actual beer that I remember drinking was at a very young age, maybe eight years old. I remember my uncle giving me what I thought was soda, but as I chugged it I realized it tasted different. It most certainly could have been beer, but I am not absolutely positive. The first actual beer that I know I drank for a certainty was at my eighth grade graduation party. I drank one Coors Light beer and remember I didn't like the taste that much; however, I was so proud of myself for finishing it that I kept the empty beer can on top of my dresser in my bedroom. It was a sign that yes, this is proof that I drank a beer, and it gave me a sense of solidarity that I was escaping from middle school to the high school era.

As a freshman in high school, I didn't really think about alcohol and partying all that much. I didn't really have an interest, but I knew there was always going to be that time that would creep up when the thought of experimentation would arise. I remember being in study hall when some of my friends asked if they could come over my house and drink some beers. Pranam, my best friend to this day, would try to persuade me, knowing that my parents wouldn't be home; they would be bartending. I decided to give into the temptation and the slogan "sure, why the hell not?" So here I was 14 or 15 years old, and I found a way to get a 30 pack of beer. It wasn't that difficult to get beer, since I knew older people who knew older people. My older brother Ryan was a junior at the same high school, so I really just needed to ask him, and he usually could get me any alcohol I wanted. The whole idea and plan came through, and a couple of my friends and I, including Pranam, began drinking at my house. The taste of beer wasn't that satisfying, but I remember the effects of feeling lively, and that warm buzz, were enough that I wanted to drink more than one.

After drinking a couple beers, my friends and I decided to try smoking marijuana. Having that buzzed feeling, we all agreed, since it seemed right in this so-called experimentation process. We smoked with my brother and one of his friends. I don't really remember the actual effects of the marijuana, but I remember walking down the street with my buddies feeling on top of the world. In a sense, I guess that term of feeling "high" could fit the description quite well.

I think I drank about a total of six beers, and when I woke up in the morning I didn't feel like my normal self. I also had to work at McDonald's that morning, which was also my first real job. About an hour or two into work I asked a coworker what a good way to get sent home would be, without getting fired, of course. The final decision was to go to the bathroom and come back acting sick, and that's exactly what I did. I walked up to one of my managers and said that I had just vomited in the bathroom and didn't feel good. The manager agreed to send me home, but I could tell she was mad, and probably even thought I was faking. Nonetheless, I felt like shit, and schemed my way out of working the rest of my shift. Looking back, I realized that the whole "do what I want" mentality would stem from that first hangover.

Walking into school Monday, after that first actual encounter with alcohol and marijuana, I felt like a changed person. In a way, in all honesty, I felt a little bit "cooler" in the social sense of the word. I was excited to talk to my friends about our time partying and discuss upcoming plans to do the same thing. From then on I had the mindset of getting together with friends and drinking on the weekends. This wouldn't occur every weekend, but when the opportunities arose we wouldn't hesitate to have a good time. I remember going to parties with upper-class men, and that in itself was a great confidence booster for a high school kid.

After trying beer, I thought it was only right to experiment with liquor. I recall vodka being the main choice of beverage. I also remember, at times, taking straight shots with a chaser of soda. I realized that the coveted "buzzed" effect would happen quicker, with less of a hassle. I figured swigging some vodka rather than drinking a six pack of beer would be more efficient.

If you drank in high school, it didn't matter if you were a freshman or a senior, everyone knew it was like that. However, I would soon learn how straight liquor can impair the human body and remove any form of self control.

The weekend of one of my friend's birthday party was coming up and I certainly wanted to celebrate. My friend's name was Josh, but he had a one-of-a-kind nickname. He was known as "Perv." I'm not going to get into the details of how he got that nickname because it's irrelevant. However, I'm sure some of my friends who are reading this right now are laughing their asses off.

I ended up getting a liter of vodka and I remember hiding the bottle in a blanket, putting it in the back of my father's truck. Since I told him I would be sleeping over at a friend's house, I figured I could pull off the stealth move, which worked without a problem. My father dropped me off at my friend's and I stepped out of the truck. Most people know of an appetizer called "pigs-in-a-blanket." Well, here I was grabbing my "vodka-in-a-blanket," saying goodbye to my father, and entering my friend's house with one intention: to get drunk.

I began drinking right away, since I wanted to feel that buzzed sensation. Once the feeling came, I began drinking more and more to intensify the effect, and before the night ended I was in my first total blackout. I remember waking up on my friend's basement floor in my own urine, slurring my words as I was still pretty intoxicated. After finding out from my friends what happened, I couldn't believe what I did. They said I was drinking vodka straight out of the bottle like it was water. Now that's a pretty scary thing, not knowing what I'd been doing and continuing to drink into oblivion. Michael Jordan was my role model, and when my friends asked me what his jersey number was, I couldn't give the correct answer. I would just slur off random numbers like "One hundred and ninety-four thousand, six hundred and twenty-one." Now that's beyond drunk. Being a young teenager, I didn't really think anything of it, but looking back now, that surely was a sign of trouble to come.

I carried on drinking as a routine on weekends through my freshman year of high school. It was during this time when the Bump, as we called it, developed into our party spot. When I say "our," I'm referring to the main group of friends with whom I hung out. This group of friends, also known as the Crew, was a tight group of friends who had each other's back. They also knew how to party and drink some booze. The Crew consisted of Pranam, Jake, Nick, John, Mitch B., Brendan, and Mike.

Getting back to the Bump, it was located right across the street from my parents' house in a huge field. It was basically a nice spot to have a fire at night and drink. It had a huge rock that people could sit on as well. The funny part was that my friends, Pranam, Nick, and Jake, also lived on the outside boarders of the Bump, so we all were in walking distance to our parents' houses at our party location. We were a couple years away from getting our driver's licenses, so the fact that we had a place we could walk to and enjoy ourselves at was beneficial in that sense. What a prime time spot the Bump was!

There did come a time when I didn't drink for a while. I was on the junior varsity basketball team during my freshman year, and towards the end of the season I had to miss our last couple games due to the surgical procedure on my chest. I remember getting a basketball signed by my teammates wishing me well, which was a thoughtful gesture. Some of my teammates used to call me "SKAB," short for "skin and bones," and although they had the right intention wishing me "Good luck, SKAB," I still had that insecurity of being the skinny kid.

The surgery was a success, although I felt the wrath of the worst pain in my life, as I mentioned earlier. I was in the hospital for about a week, and the only thing keeping the pain tolerable was the morphine pump. I clicked that button as often as I could, but I later found out that the machine would only give you a certain amount of medicine within a certain timeframe. When I was released from the hospital I spent the next month or so home, where I also completed the schoolwork I would be missing from my leave of absence. I mentioned earlier that I did not take any pain medication during my stay at home, although I was in severe pain. I know I was prescribed Oxycontin, but back then I didn't even know what that was. It's crazy because I had no idea that the nightmare of pain medication would catch up to me later on in life.

I didn't realize my first incident with the law would come into play during my sophomore year of high school. I had a Spanish teacher who wasn't your typical "professional" teacher. During class we were given freedoms other teachers would never allow. I remember one class where this teacher closed the doors of the classroom and we were allowed to listen to Godsmack on the classroom's CD player. There was another time where I had brought up my test to the teacher and she said she had a picture of me by her bed that she fell asleep to every night. I found out that day that this teacher had been having parties at her house throughout the school year and had been drinking with students from the high school. When I discovered the news, a couple friends and I decided to go to one of her parties after the school bonfire that night. These friends were Chris, Nick, Jake, and Brendan.

When we arrived at the Spanish teacher's house, I noticed students from my high school were already there drinking. It was said that she had had parties before and that she also had sexual intercourse with students from my high school. It didn't really appear to be a problem being at my teacher's house, but the main concern at the time was that we needed alcohol. We didn't hesitate to ask the teacher, and she agreed to go to the liquor store and buy us alcohol. So here we were, a bunch of high school students left alone at our teacher's house partying while her two- or three-year-old son gazed at us.

Our teacher finally returned with our alcohol: a couple six-packs of Smirnoff Ice and a bottle of Captain Morgan's. I began to indulge in the alcoholic beverages and socialize with everybody. I noticed that our teacher was a bit of a wild woman, as she and a student began to wrestle for fun in her living room while her toddler looked on. As my buzz started to kick in, my friends agreed it would be a good time to leave the teacher's house and head over to the high school dance. We walked out the door and soon were approached by a woman who would later be identified as a probation officer. She was investigating hints that recent parties involving students of the school had been thrown at that teacher's house.

Since we were carrying alcohol out of the house, it gave the probation officer probable cause to stop us. She asked us to drop the alcohol, give our names (Nick giving a fake name!), and we were soon on our way to the local police station. Once we arrived at the police station we all darted to the bathroom at once to urinate. After we were finished, we each had to take a breathalyzer test for our blood alcohol content. I recall my BAC was .08, and I definitely felt more than buzzed. The police officer asked if I wanted to call my parents to fill them in on the situation, and I just remember being scared to death to call them. I had the police officer call my house phone, but my parents weren't around. The next option was to call my uncle, of all people, who was the superintendent of the school district at the time. They reached my uncle and he picked me up at the police station. Since my parents were working, my uncle brought me to his house, where I anxiously awaited my parents arrival. When my parents finally confronted me, they were both very disappointed. It was in fact the first time I had been in serious trouble, and I knew there would be consequences, since this would turn into a legal matter.

Before I was able to rejoin my high school (I believe I was suspended for one or two days), I had to sit down with my parents and the high school principal and explain my involvement in the matter, along with all the details of what occurred that night. As for the legal matters, I was ordered 25 hours of community service and had to attend an alcohol/drug program at the high school. I'm not sure if I was put on probation, since I was a minor, but I did have to testify in court, which was one of the toughest things I ever had to face at that point in my life. Here I was, 15 years old, sitting in front of a full courtroom and a group of jurors. Here I was testifying my involvement to help determine my Spanish teacher's potential fate. I was being cross-examined and the whole nine yards, but I got through it. The whole trial took about a week or two, and the teacher was sent to jail for six months. Her teaching career was over. I felt a sense of relief when the trial was finally over.

Looking back I remember that I didn't take this whole trial and legal issue as an area of concern with regard to my future of high school drinking. In all seriousness, why would I? I made a mistake. It was a poor judgment call on my behalf. I admit that it was an idiotic move, but how the hell was I supposed to know there would be a probation officer watching the house? People always like to use the phrase "live and learn," and as you will find out, I seemed to end up always learning the hard way. We all make mistakes in life, and sometimes it takes people a long time to get the big picture. Others may never learn. As for myself, I guess you can say I'm fortunate, to put it frankly. I fell down so many damn times in life that I thought I'd never get up again. But I did.

The big picture was there, I just couldn't see it. I was still in high school and I was still going to drink. After the trial was over, I didn't get right back into drinking. I took a little time for reflection. I remember a couple of my friends who were involved in the trial were grounded for quite a while. My parents never grounded me. At least that's what I thought. It's not like I was locked inside my house or told I couldn't come out of my room to use the computer. I still had freedoms that my friends didn't. I guess my parents thought this whole incident was a fluke, which in reality was how I pictured it too. I was in a fact a good student and took my studies seriously, so I understand why my parents weren't so hard on me. Should they have been? I would say yes, but it was my mentality that I wouldn't let this kind of thing happen again. If they did have a harsher punishment, I probably would have talked my way out of it. It wasn't until a few weekends later when I began to drink again. I drank because it was high school. I drank because it was socially acceptable. I drank because I liked it. Of course there was some peer pressure involved, but nobody was forcing booze down my throat except me.

Growing up, there was always alcohol in the house. Both my parents drank, and I had never seen alcohol to be an interfering problem for them. They both drink socially, but never relied on alcohol like I have. I remember alcohol being easily accessible at my house, so I did what seemed to be an undercover move. I would often steal liquor out of the bottle and then fill up what I took out with water. I was only 15 or 16 years old. Could this be a sign of worse things to come? Of course I thought nothing of it. I just wanted to get a buzz and hang out with my friends.

Although I did not drink during the week, I often did on the weekends throughout my sophomore year of high school. Besides the occasional partying, I was staying out of trouble and it was actually turning out to be a breakthrough year for me. Halfway through the basketball season as a junior varsity player, I was moved up to the varsity squad mainly because of my shooting ability. During my middle school days I was considered one of the best three-point shooters in the county, and I continued to improve that ability throughout my high school years. I think making 14 three-pointers within two games caught the coach's attention. Anyways, I remember the next practice we had I was still on J.V. and I was asked to practice with the varsity team. They had me run this play where I would come off a screen to get an open three-point shot. To make the story short, we ran the play five or six times and I didn't miss. The next day I came into practice and the J.V. coach asked why I showed up to the gym so early. I said that I was there to practice with the J.V. team, and that's when I heard the news that I was officially a part of the varsity basketball team. I remember how excited and proud I was. I was especially excited to inform my parents of the news, who were great supporters throughout my youth days in sports. It was great to see that my hard work paid off and my talent was noticed.

I remember my first game on the varsity team as a sophomore was one of the highlights of my career. We were on our home court and running through the entrance of fervent cheerleaders to start warming up. It was a moment of glory. Our entrance music and the volume of the enthusiastic fans was more than enough to get us pumped up. Our basketball program has always been very competitive and well respected in Berkshire County (Hoosac Valley is a Division II high school).

The game began and I was put in midway through the first half. I wasn't really nervous but I remember receiving a pass and as I prepared to shoot my three-point shot, I noticed an extended hand attempt to block my shot. Luckily, I had enough time to catch and release the ball over the extended hand and it traveled through the air, hitting nothing but the bottom of the net. The crowd erupted with cheer and I was just happy to be on the court. Being a part of the team had a sense of fulfillment in itself and making my first shot was frosting on the cake. It was a high point of my life, which I thought would carry over as a clear path to more progress. However, we all seem to cross a bump in the road from time to time. My bump turned out to be bigger than usual.

This so called "big bump in the road" occurred during my senior year of high school. It was October 18, 2003 and I continued my regular weekend drinking routine throughout my sophomore year up until this date. The event occurred during a weekend night and I was at my friend's house. We were looking for alcohol and couldn't find anybody to buy it for us at that particular time. Somehow I came across some vodka and I made the stiffest drink imaginable. So as you could imagine, the drink consisted mainly of straight vodka, with a splash of soda. I drank it down and was feeling good. Meanwhile everybody wanted to go to another friend's house. I was asked if I wanted a ride, but I said that I was all right to drive. I got behind the wheel and made it safely to another friend's house where there was alcohol available. Of course I went right for the vodka and began drinking it straight out of the bottle. As the night progressed my friend Libby asked if I would drive her to the store to get cigarettes. Being the confident "drunk" that I was, I agreed. Poor judgment arises when alcohol consumes the body, especially at the beginning stages of anyone's drinking career.

Walking out of my friend's house to get into the driver's seat for a second time, I was unaware of the consequences that would come about as a result of this "poor judgment" decision. As I arrived at the store, Libby walked out with her cigarettes and as she sat in the passenger seat I drove back towards the party. Shortly after getting back on the road I could feel the effects of alcohol creep up and distort my inhibitions. Not in the right state of mind, I began to lose sight of the road. I veered to the side of the street and crashed into a parked car. After impact I asked, "What happened?" and Libby replied, "You just fucking crashed into a parked car!" The passenger window was smashed and my friend crawled through the window and fled the scene. There were no serious injuries to us. We were lucky and just had some bumps and bruises.

Once Libby left I knew I was busted and decided to wait inside my vehicle until the cops arrived. Probably the smartest decision I made that horrible night. The cop arrived and asked me to step out of my vehicle where he asked if I had any injuries. I said that I was fine and he continued to give me a field sobriety test. The moment I began to walk the straight line, it was evident that I needed to be placed into handcuffs. My version of walking a straight line that night could be compared to a dysfunctional member of the marching band.

I was now handcuffed, sitting in the back of a police car,

being transported to the local police station. Upon arrival the police officer instructed that I take a breathalyzer test, which measures one's blood alcohol concentration (BAC). I agreed and my BAC read .24, which was three times the legal limit. The sad part was I wasn't even legal to drink. For Christ sakes, I wasn't even the legal age to smoke cigarettes. I was 17. After the process with the courts ended I had a DUI on my record. I was put on probation and lost my driving privileges for one year. I also had to attend and complete an alcohol education program. Since the incident occurred right before the start of my senior basketball season, I was stripped of my title as captain. However, I was lucky to even play.

I remember how awful I felt the next day after my DUI arrest. I literally stayed in bed all day. The last thing I wanted to do was face the world. When I finally managed to get out of bed my mother told me that life was going to suck for a while. A tear ran down my face as I knew my mother was right. My car was towed to my house and was placed in my front yard. It was meant to be seen by the students sitting on the bus when it drove by my house Monday morning. They would be able to witness the wreckage along with any other passersby. Picture a red Plymouth Neon, cut the car in half, and remove the entire hood inward, stopping right before the windshield. It was a horrific image and getting away with minor bumps and bruises was a Godsend. It was a Godsend that I didn't kill my friend in the passenger seat or any other innocent bystander that could have fallen victim that night. I was incredibly lucky. I was alive and nobody was seriously hurt. Nobody was dead. Did I learn my lesson? Did I at least look at the fact that maybe this was a wake-up call and I should stop indulging in alcohol? Of course I did, but I was a senior in high school and completely letting go of alcohol wasn't an option for me.

I was a senior ready to start the basketball season. I remember after I got my DUI charge my parents, and even Pranam, who was my teammate at the time, encouraged me to call my basketball coach and inform him of the incident. Weeks went by and I never built up the courage to call him. I just couldn't do it. I regret it to this day because the first official practice we had my coach asked me to stay back to talk to him. He said, "Skrock, why didn't you call me about the incident? I wanted to hear it from you before I read it in the newspaper." Right then and there he stripped me of my title as captain. Maybe things could have been different if I had had the courage. I was fortunate to play and my coach was lenient. I had to attend an alcohol class every Tuesday evening during our practice time. Thankfully, our games never fell on a Wednesday, otherwise I wouldn't be able to start, as I would be missing a practice the day before a game. I really didn't have it "that bad."

I was able to start every game, and the season was one of the most memorable times of my life. During my junior year our team won the school's first ever Western Massachusetts Division II Championship. The game was won on the campus of UMass, Amherst at Curry Hicks Cage where the legend Dr. Julius Erving played his college ball. We won the game on a buzzer beater layup, and that moment of glory couldn't be taken from us. It was sheer pandemonium as the crowd rushed the court. It was the kind of high that no alcohol or drug could compete against. Just one of those once in a lifetime kind of feelings. Our team bus was escorted by police cruisers and fire trucks all the way back to our hometown of Adams, Massachusetts, where we took a final victory lap. The support was as good as it gets. People were cheering in their front yards hooting, hollering, and raising self-made banners. In all honesty, I'd rather stay in that moment all day and night. However, the curse of alcohol and celebration seemed to get in the way. It was impossible to refuse that curse on a day like that. We later won our next game at the Mullins Center at UMass, and moved on to the state finals at the Worcester Centrum. We ended up losing in the state finals to a ridiculously gifted Charlestown team, which transferred to a Division I team the following year.

We started off the season with five wins and eight losses during my senior year. It wasn't a surprising comeback from being previously named the second best team in the State of Massachusetts in Division II. I remember my teammates and I just clowning around at practice because we thought we were unworthy. All of a sudden something just clicked. It's amazing sometimes when you just find that rhythm and that unity as a team. We weren't being selfish. We started looking out for one another and didn't bring anybody down, on or off the court. We were finally a team. We were a team that was determined to win and something just clicked. We needed ten wins to get into the Western Mass Tournament and we won our final seven games. We ended up getting home court advantage and would play our quarterfinal game against a strong Southwick team. This game would turn out to be the most memorable and inspiring games of my basketball career, hands down.

I remember Pranam and I went to church before our game. I'm glad we did. It was like this spiritual awakening leading up to the game. As I sat in the locker room before the game started I closed my eyes and just visualized myself shooting and scoring. Our team then gathered in the locker room and we huddled around each other swaying back and forth to the song "I believe I can Fly" by R. Kelly. If that isn't team unity, I don't know what is.

It was finally game time and it took a little while to get into the flow of the game. I made two three-pointers in the first half and we were basically trading baskets at best. We never really got control of the game. It didn't help when an opposing player made nearly a half-court shot to end the first half. It was evident that the momentum of the game was not in our favor. It seemed as if we lost some confidence, but I knew we weren't going to give up.

Southwick was in total control in the second half as they increased their lead to 16 points with about ten minutes left. We seniors had our basketball careers on the line. Then something clicked. We didn't want to walk off our home court with our heads down, and we most certainly didn't want to lose without putting up a fight. We began to chip away at the score in incremental amounts, bit by bit. It was as if we were climbing a mountain in a hailstorm and treading our way to the top.

We managed to dwindle the score and found ourselves down by two points with about a minute left in the game. We had the ball and Skiff, as we called him, made a three-pointer and we now had the lead. The gymnasium completely erupted with cheer; I never felt such adrenaline flow through my veins. The game still wasn't over, Southwick had possession, but our intense and smart defense stopped them. Coming back on offense, we ran some time off the clock when the ball was passed to me from the inside to the corner for a three-point shot. I did not hesitate and I shot the ball. Nothing but net, nail in the coffin. We were now up by four points with about 20 seconds left. I thought the gymnasium itself was jumping up and down, the fans just erupted. Pranam jumped on my back, cheering with joy. I never before and never again felt that sense of amazement and energy in my entire career. So many emotions were running through that "Home of the Hurricanes" gym. We ended up winning the game, and washed away Southwick, as true Hurricanes do.

I'm not going to get into much detail about the final game of my high school basketball career, other than we lost. I got elbowed early in the game and was bleeding all over the court, trying to hide the blood when finally I almost vomited blood and took myself out of the game. From that moment I was knocked off my game, and it sucked. My teammates played their asses off and we had the game in the books until an opposing player from South Hadley hit a three-pointer to take the lead near the end of the game. From there we lost control of the game and our season ended. Of course we wanted to win and have another shot at the Western Mass title, but we left the "Cage" with no regrets. It was a memorable and successful season that

I can always look back on. It was a season that went from no hope, to all the hope in the world. As I said before, it was a season that just "clicked."

I wanted to include my senior basketball season in my story because it portrays a lot of where I was and where I am now from a recovery standpoint. That sense of "no hope to all the hope in the world" is a true perception of myself as an alcoholic and addict in recovery. I remember when I got home from the Southwick game, my grandparents were there since my parents were on vacation out of the country. The first thing I wanted to do was find some alcohol to celebrate the victory. I went down into my basement to see if I could sneak some beers out of the fridge to bring to my friend's house. The moment I open the fridge I hear my grandmother, also known as my Babci, holler "Trev, you better not be taking any alcohol!" My family knew I drank, I knew that. But the funny part is why were my grandparents at my house in the first place? Were they there to congratulate me after the best game of my career? Or were they there to keep an eye on me and make sure I didn't throw a party at my parents' house, which I was well known to do? The main reason they were there was because I couldn't be trusted. Hell, even I knew that.

I obviously never had a good grip on my drinking throughout high school. I would throw parties at my parents' house whenever I had the opportunity. Whether they would be out of town for the weekend or coming back late the same night, I always managed to have people over to drink. This happened quite often throughout high school, and the scary part is that my poor decisions put my parents in a tough position every time. Basically everybody that I had at my parties was underage, therefore if something serious happened, my parents would be held responsible. I can't count how many times they specifically told me not to have anybody over to drink. The fact of the matter was that I didn't care. I was selfish and I always gave in to my friends. If they wanted to drink and my house was available, for the most part, I wouldn't back down. I am very fortunate nothing serious ever happened, because throughout the years there were many underage people who decided to get into their vehicles and leave my house intoxicated. Putting a burden like that upon my parents is such an irresponsible move. And I wonder why they never trusted me. I never blamed them for it—how could I? The best way to cover up the guilt would be to drink, and that's exactly what I did.

How crazy stupid was I, anyway? My parents' house resides on one of the main roads in Adams, and you wouldn't believe the number of vehicles that would be parked outside when I intended to have a big party. I remember one party in particular where I must have had 70 people over. There were vehicles lined up and down East Road on both sides of the street. To make things even riskier, there's a state trooper that lives a few houses down the street. I don't know how I never got busted.

The fact of the matter was, if I didn't get busted, I would continue to throw parties. It's kind of how alcoholics and addicts think, such as if they never got pulled over for drinking or drugging, they would continue the same behavior and get behind the wheel while doing so. I know that's what I did. Unfortunately, I had to learn the hard way, as you will later find out in my story. I will portray a trend that will unfold in my alcoholic/addiction related actions.

High school was coming to a close, and my friends and I graduated, pursuing our last summer before most of us awaited our journey into the college atmosphere. Of course we all wanted to get together as much as possible during the summer to party. I began to grow a stronger relationship with alcohol and simply enjoyed its effects. I began to grow a tolerance to alcohol as well, as I had consistently chosen to drink liquor over beer. I mean I still drank beer, but I would much rather drink liquor. It was quicker, everyone knows that! I only had a few times where I had those blackout nights. You know that stage where you're so intoxicated that you have no idea what you're doing, but you're still awake and somewhat functioning? It definitely happened to me, just not consistently. I preferred to get as drunk as I could and be able to still enjoy the party. I was real fucking good at that. Being as skinny as I was, I could drink a lot of my friends under the table. In fact, people were like "Skrock, how the fuck are you still functioning?" I guess it was a talent, kind of like my three-point shot, both entertaining in their own way. I tried to control the way I drank, and make alcohol my bitch, per say. I soon found out that we were friends, we were enemies, we were unpredictable. I smoked marijuana at times, but it wasn't something that I'd spend my money on. I would smoke if my friends had it and I was feeling up to it.

My senior skip day party was a great time. Well, it started out as a great time, for me at least. The ending wasn't really in my plan, but hey, shit happens when you drink to excess. Like I said before, most of the parties that happened during high school occurred outdoors around a fire in the middle of the woods. So our senior class planned this party accordingly. We found a prime location in Savoy, if I'm not mistaken, which is a pretty desolate area surrounded by woods. So it was perfect for a bunch of eager high school seniors to get a little rowdy. We brought pallets upon pallets to burn. Pallets were actually a necessity for parties; they would keep the fire going for a while. Especially if you had about 30 of them. So we had everything planned and it was time to party.

Me and my buddy Nick got ourselves two 30 packs of beer, just in case. We figured 30 beers a piece would do the trick because it wasn't a bad idea to have that safety net of extra alcohol. I drank and I drank and I drank some more. I always had a beer in my hand that night, my main focus on getting as fucked up as possible without actually blacking out. Well, I can say I made it pretty damn far into the night remembering everything until the alcohol took control. I don't know how and I don't know why, but I ended up waking up on a tiny wooden spool in the middle of the woods where we had our fire. I got up, looked around and there was nobody in sight. My calves we covered with mosquito bites. And when I say covered, let's just say they had a feasting on my legs. It was such an awful feeling and the image of my legs at the time was grotesque. It took over a month for my legs to actually heal. It really sucked.

So here I am in the middle of the woods with nobody in sight, covered in mosquito bites, not to mention still drunk, and a park ranger comes walking over towards me. He's like, "What happened here?", my response being, "Oh nothing really, just had a little party with some friends last night." He says, "Well you can't be doing this out here. Pick up this mess before you leave." It was then that I actually looked around my surroundings and saw a gigantic fire pit with about four feet of ashes. There were beer cans, bottles, and trash everywhere. I was like "What the fuck? You have got to be kidding me!" I had no idea where anybody was, I was hoping this park ranger dude would just leave. Luckily he did, and I began to search the perimeter of the woods looking for any of my friends. I finally found a truck parked a little ways outside of our party spot and it was my friend Chad's. I was like, "Thank God!" I hopped in the bed of his truck and he brought me home. Fuck picking up the trash, I had mosquito bites to tend to.

I did pretty well throughout my high school career and ended up in the mid 80s for a final average, which wasn't bad at all. I didn't make honors, but I was almost there, just behind a few points. There was a time for studying and a time for partying. I made sure I took my school work seriously, and I did my best. I have no regrets on my efforts in high school, and my experience as a whole. The DUI sucked, but it didn't ruin my attempt to get good grades and get into a good college. My SAT scores were awful, though. I couldn't take that test for the life of me, and that pissed me off. It sucked that colleges implemented those scores on such a great scale from an acceptance standpoint. I did not get into my top choice of schools, but I ended up getting into a prestigious private school.

I attended Franklin Pierce College (today it's known as Franklin Pierce University) in the fall of 2004, majoring in Sports Management. The college is located in Rindge, NH which is pretty much in the middle of nowhere. So here I am, a top notch high school drinker coming into this college, which isn't that well known to be a party school. I mean it was no UMass. As move-in day arrived, I went up with one of my high school friends and met another high school friend at the college. John and Mitch W. were going to be my roommates, which was definitely a sense of relief coming into this new chapter of life. I wasn't really afraid of making friends, it just took me some time. Having John and Mitch there, the kids with whom I grew up from childhood to present day, was reassuring.

I remember move-in day quite well. After getting all of our belongings to the dorm room, we patiently waited for our parents to leave so we could finally start our college journey on our own. We would be in control of our own decision making, and although I was still on probation and had to meet with a counselor at the college (from my prior DUI in high school), I was still apt to drink. When our parents finally left, I remember Mitch looking everywhere for a half gallon of vodka which he brought to the dorm undercover. It was nowhere to be found and the only conclusion was that his parents had found it. We were left without any booze and were unable to celebrate at the time. Back then it wasn't really a big deal to me. It wasn't like I was an alcoholic and needed a drink right then and there. I didn't drink every day, although I probably would have if alcohol presented itself to me every day.

It was, in fact, a mission in itself to actually get alcohol while at Franklin Pierce. We really didn't have any reliable connections at the college. I mean there were times where we asked and got lucky here and there, but other than that we had to come up with a way to provide ourselves with alcohol. It was basically Mitch and I who enjoyed drinking, and John was perfectly fine with smoking marijuana. I smoked pot on occasion, but it really wasn't my cup of tea at that point of my life. It was fun to go on burn cruises (smoking weed while going for a cruise in the car) every now and then. My roommates would take advantage of this option at every opportunity. I'm not judging them because I'm not a judgmental person. I never was and I never plan to be. They were the nicest, funniest kids. I would just rather drink.

So going back to our alcohol finding mission, we really had one of two options. Since Mitch usually went home on the weekends, I would go with him because there wasn't really a party life going on at the college. I would try to get alcohol when I was back in my hometown and bring it back to college with me. The other option to obtain alcohol was easy. Mitch was able to purchase alcohol at a particular package store. From his appearance, he looked over 21, so the owners knew him and never carded him. So if we were at school and wanted alcohol we would often take the hour and a half drive just to get it. That was our last resort, and we would often take that drive because when we were home for the weekend we would leave at 5 A.M. on Monday morning in order for him to get to his first class on time. That particular package store wouldn't be open at that hour.

Looking back, I guess I was just gearing up to handle this college life the best way I knew how. It's crazy because I was at the stage where I was looking ahead and planning how and when I could get alcohol. I mean I remember sitting down at my desk during the week and making a "booze list" that I would bring home with me. I felt a sense of empowerment, like I could magically make alcohol present itself. All I had to do was make this list and pass it off to one of the many people I knew who were reliable "purchasers for the under-aged drinkers of America."

I still took college seriously. I did all my homework, studied my ass off and made the dean's list. I was a smart college student, but not a very bright individual. I was taking all the risks in the world, being on probation for alcohol related incidents and all. I would sneak alcohol in our dorm, drink, and not think of any consequences. I mean, who was going to bust me? I never wanted to start trouble when I drank, I just wanted to have a good time.

There was one particular incident that occurred during my freshman year at Franklin Pierce that proved to be another sign of my poor judgment calls. Of course I carried the mentality that I would never get caught doing something illegal on campus. Boy did my mentality get in the way. I always had the notion that if I got away with it before, then I would get away with it again. However, that particular night, a couple buddies and I went out to buy a few 30 packs of beer. When we returned back to campus we had to develop a plan to transport the 30 packs into our dorm. We decided that we would leave the beer in the car and get a few duffle bags from our rooms so we could hide the beer inside. Right before we walked back outside with our empty duffle bags, we noticed a Residential Adviser on the bottom floor watching us. However, we thought nothing of it and carried on with the plan. As we walked back inside through the bottom floor entrance, the RA was still there and she stopped us. She had a suspicion that we had something we weren't supposed to have in our bags. I'm pretty sure she noticed our empty bags when we left, and within a couple minutes, there we were returning with full bags of who knows what, which gave her reason to search.

My buddies and I complied with the RA and our 30 packs of beer were discovered. We were asked to take all the beer back outside in the freezing cold and open each beer can individually, pouring its contents onto the ground, and dispose the cans into the dumpster. We had no choice but to do just that. Talk about disappointment! I think we had at least four 30 packs, so that's 120 cans of beer. That's a lot of beer to crack open with your frozen fingers, even between three people. It gave us a sense that we had lost the battle, but not the war. Here comes that mentality of mine again, which seemed to never go away! You now have three pissed off college freshman who spent about an hour outside in the freezing cold pouring out their liquid courage because their so-called "superhuman" mentalities got in the way. Well, at least mine did. It was just plain old bullshit in my eyes. I spend all week working my ass off in the classrooms and this bitch is going to bust my balls over a night of celebration? I think not. I could give two shits about what was going to happen to me, being on probation and all, and seeing this counselor at the college and everything. I wasn't about to think about the consequences at the time the incident occurred. Of course it was in the back of my head. I would say that this incident actually got the pot stirring between Trevor Skrocki, the good student and Trevor Skrocki, the party animal. It was the beginning to a long-lasting, dreadful relationship with my so-called guilty conscience.

The question was how was I going to go about this situation I was in? The answer was plain and simple. I was back off campus with my buddy right back to the supermarket where we previously purchased our beer. Only this time, we purchased five 30 packs of beer (even though my buddy wasn't 21 years old, he knew a worker who let us buy the beer), which was ultimately our entitlement of revenge towards our previous encounter with discouragement. Basically, my decision was to rub it in. If you're going to put me through the anguish of pouring out 120 beers, I'm going to come back with 150 beers and attempt to drown out the humiliation with self-satisfaction. We succeeded in getting the shit ton of full beer cans, our new prized possessions, into the dorm, and we got drunk. However, I still had that son of a bitch guilty conscience to deal with. At this point, I could have been featured in an Eminem music video.

I woke up the next morning, obviously hungover. All I could think was "What's going to happen to me now?" I tried to just brush the whole incident aside and act as if nothing happened.

But you know how colleges are with their zero tolerance policies. I knew it wouldn't just go away, so I played the whole sitting and waiting game. The next thing I know, there is a knock at the door a few days later, and it's the RA. She said that I was to meet with the counselor I had been seeing at the college. I am almost positive that I drank after I heard that news. I didn't know what was going to happen, so why not drink? Real smart, I thought. Through the years, I've found that you can only calm the nerves so much by drinking alcohol. In the predicament I was in, drinking only made me stress out more.

The following day arrived and I met with my counselor. The moment I walked in to sit down and meet with him I saw sheer disappointment across his face. Now you also have to realize that this guy wasn't a professional drug and alcohol counselor. I forget his actual title at the college, but he might have been the vice president, if I'm not mistaken — a real cool dude. He was always in my corner and on my side when I met with him in the past. He was rooting for me and just wanted me to have a successful freshman year at the school. When I saw that disappointed look on his face, I felt like I had let a strong supporter down.

He was disappointed in the fact that he heard about the incident from a source other than myself. It was as if I was in the same predicament all over again. Didn't I do the same thing to my high school basketball coach? Not owning up to my mistake and having him read it in the newspaper? I was basically repeating the same fuck ups because I didn't have the courage to own up to them. I didn't want that reputation of being the troubled kid, because I felt like I was, in fact, a downright good person at heart. It wasn't my intention to get caught, but trouble always seemed to follow me when alcohol or drugs were involved.

I felt like I really let this guy down. Here he was taking time out of his day to talk to me and attest to the guidelines of my probation, and I totally just fucked him over. He even told me that he was filling in other facilitators and associated members of the college that he was meeting one-on-one with a bright kid. He seemed grateful to be helping me out and now his disappointment and my shame created turmoil in our relationship. I guess you could say that I couldn't be trusted. Without trust, it's tough to maintain a strong relationship, and the sad part is I gave up. Fortunately, he decided not to tell my probation officer of the incident and told me that I was in charge of my own choices going forward. I never went to go see him again. I was just happy and relieved that the terms of my probation weren't affected. Do you think I learned my lesson? Of course I did. I said, "Trevor, just try to be a little more careful next time!" I was a freshman in college, for crying out loud. I wasn't about to give up partying that easily.

One weekend at Franklin Pierce we had planned a trip to the strip club nearby. It was John, Mitch and myself. There might have been another person or two, but I'm not sure. I remember drinking straight blackberry brandy and Captain Morgan's. It's not a pleasant combination, especially if you're drinking these liquors straight. I was so geared and ready to go that by the time we got to the strip club, I never made it inside. I was left in the car passed out with my head against the front passenger floor and my feet up in the air towards the seat. Now, I know that I'm 100% Polish, but damn. What a sight that must have been. My friends later told me that one of the workers in the strip club was keeping an eye on me as I scrambled around the vehicle. It must have looked like I was playing Twister inside the little car. In my opinion, I was just completely hammered, probably imagining that I was on a different planet. Alcohol had taken control of me again.

There was also this time when John and I went off campus for a cruise to get some food. We went with another friend of ours, Greg, who brought along some marijuana and a nice looking bowl piece. I wasn't planning on smoking, but when the opportunity arose I changed my mind. I took a few rips and I was stoned off my ass. Higher than I had ever been in my entire life. When we got to the drive-through of KFC I began to freak out. It was crazy, I mean everything just kept repeating. I told John what I wanted, I put my hand in my pocket to reach for money, and then Greg would look back at me from the passenger seat with the same grin on his face. Everything kept repeating and it felt as if time was just stuck. Like we all were stuck in this moment forever. It was crazy because you have John and Greg who are laughing, but everything keeps repeating exactly the same. They kept laughing, but the time didn't seem to move forward. I really thought that time was stuck, as if I was locked in a repeating cycle of actions. I finally was able to pull a few dollars out of my pocket after numerous attempts, and we got our food. Time was finally moving and I grew back a little bit of sanity. On the ride back to campus, I was sitting in the back seat of the car and my heart was pounding. I thought it was going to pop out of my chest. I thought something bad was happening to me. Luckily, we got back to campus and I made it into our dorm room. I got on my bed and began to freak out again. I was frightened, my heart was racing, and I asked John to call 9-1-1. I thought I was having a heart attack. John talked me down and told me to relax and eat some food. I did and I finally started to feel somewhat normal. It was by far one of the scariest encounters I ever experienced. I swear that weed was laced with something.

I tended to go home on the weekends to party, rather than staying at the college. It was a really boring college. I'm not saying it was a bad school, I excelled academically and enjoyed going to my classes. The whole party life was dull. At least at home I could party around a huge fire in the middle of the woods. That's a bit more entertaining.

I remember my friend Rachelle had a party at her parents' house in March, 2005. A lot of people came home from college for the weekend, thus a lot of my high school friends got together to party that night. It's always a good feeling to reunite and catch up with your good friends, so that party stood out for me, being a freshman in college and all. There were people who were in college, high school, or neither. There was a good mix of people there, which made the party interesting and entertaining. I always enjoyed partying with people younger and older than me. I was friends with everyone. That's just how it was. It's good knowing that when you walk into a party everyone will welcome you with open arms. Well, it was more like, "Skrock is here, Fuck yeah!" But you get the idea. I got along with everyone. I wasn't the person that started any trouble. I just wanted to get fucked up and have a good time with my friends, as you may already know by now.

The party was awesome and everyone was having fun. I remember seeing a good friend I went to high school with, Tommy Oxton. He was a one-of-a-kind individual, and it was impossible not to like him. He was such a gifted athlete throughout the years as well, and he was both a teammate and opponent of mine along our journey of competitive sports. He was a standout football and baseball player when competing at Hoosac Valley and was one of the best wrestlers Berkshire County had ever seen. Tommy was such a likable person. His kindness and sense of humor always brought joy to those around him. Plain and simple, you could always be yourself around Tommy and you always got something out of talking to him. You always walked away with something, whether it was some insight on sports, advice about life, or even a laugh: you got something and it was always positive.

I ended up sleeping at Rachelle's house because I was drunk and didn't want to take the risk of driving my car home. The first good decision I made in a while. When I woke up in the morning I still felt intoxicated. I remember walking outside to my car and the sun was beaming down into my eyes. God, my head was pounding! I drove home, and I remember seeing my mother in the kitchen. She says something like "Are you still drunk?" I'm pretty sure my response was "No," but who was I kidding? I just stumbled into my bedroom and took a nap.

After awakening from my nap I ate some dinner and went on the computer at my household. I began to read "away messages" of news that Tommy was in rough shape, not from drinking and the way I felt earlier. He had gone over to his best friend's house to get a video game. His friend's father began arguing that Tommy was spending too much time with his son. As Tommy was sitting in the vehicle's passenger seat, the father became heated and approached Tommy with a shotgun pointed in his face. Tommy pleaded for his life, and the insane man pulled the trigger. Tommy was airlifted to the hospital and fought until he could fight no more. The fact of the matter was that he was dead and I couldn't understand why.

Just like that, the news spread so quickly. I was in shock and had to find the courage to tell my parents the tragic news. I remember my mother was downstairs watching television and my father was in the other room. I decided to walk downstairs and tell my mother. I told her that I had some bad news and I just started crying. I spit the words out of what happened and began to weep. It was probably the saddest news I ever had to tell somebody. I know it was my mother that I was telling, but it didn't make a difference. By far the hardest words I ever had to speak. I can still picture myself doing it and I stand by how difficult it really was.

Moments later, my hometown friend and college roommate Mitch W. knocked on my house door. As I opened the door I saw Mitch standing there, disoriented with sadness. It was a Sunday, and we both decided to take a week off from college and stay home. We needed time to mourn the loss of our dear friend Tommy. We needed time to gather and console with friends and family. We needed time to understand why. We just needed time.

During the week, I hung out with friends as we prepared ourselves for Tommy's wake and funeral. I remember walking into his wake with a rose clenched in my hand. I went into the kneeling position by his open casket and began to pray. As I looked inside the casket at my good friend I realized that he did not look like his usual self. It was such as sad sight. For a human being that had been shot with a bullet to the face he still did, however, display a strong persona. Tommy was a warrior. On that tragic day, he clenched on to life and fought until he could fight no more. He never gave up on life. He loved life. He loved his family. He loved his friends. He wanted to become a Marine. It was a tragedy. Purely tragic.

Tommy had died a few days before my 19th birthday, so for my birthday my friends and I got together and drank. I couldn't have cared less if it was my birthday or not, I just wanted my friend back. Drinking helped mask my feelings of losing a close friend. I felt that if I drank, the sadness would leave, but it didn't. I've come to realize the only thing that helps in a tragedy such as this is time. I have grown to believe in the phrase "Time heals all wounds."

I finished up the rest of my freshman year at Franklin Pierce and had a decision to make. Mitch and John were both going to transfer to other colleges, so the question was if I was going to stay at Franklin Pierce or transfer to another school. Although it was a great private college and I excelled academically, I decided that Franklin Pierce wasn't the place for me. I would end up transferring to the University of Massachusetts, Amherst in the fall of 2005.

One of my good friends from the Crew, Brendan, also attended UMass, so it was nice going into my sophomore year knowing he would be there. UMass was a well-known party school, so it would be a complete 180 coming from Franklin Pierce. I was excited to finally see what one of the top-notch party schools was all about. Brendan was also there with his girlfriend Amanda (they are now married), with whom we went to high school, so we all knew each other well and got along great. Our weekend always started on Wednesday, or at least that's when our first initial drinking night began (for me and Brendan, anyways). We would plan on drinking Wednesday, Thursday, Friday, and Saturday every week. Sometimes not every Wednesday, but definitely on Thursday. They don't call it Thirsty Thursday for the weekly Soda-thon, do they? Because if that were the case, I totally got the wrong message. It was easier to track down alcohol as Brendon knew some people that were able to buy it for us most of the time. We definitely drank and partied a lot during the first semester at UMass, but we also took our studies seriously. I came to UMass with the same mentality as I had at Franklin Pierce and planned on doing well in all my classes. Only this time, there would be a bit more partying involved. So I had to balance my studies with my leisure time with alcohol and marijuana, and I did a damn good job. The only shitty part was being hungover at class, but I got used to it. It was that part of college to which most students had to adapt. I think I received a 3.42 GPA for the semester. Brendan probably got something like a 3.9. He was always super smart. Even in high school.

During the summer before I left for UMass, I had met with a doctor out in Boston to take a look at my back. My lower back had been in severe pain for months and months. I had been through physical therapy, but the pain wouldn't go away. The doctor had looked at my x-rays and concluded that I needed surgery. It's not like I injured my back from a previous incident, the problem had just occurred on its own. I was scheduled for surgery, and a spinal fusion was performed during my winter break from UMass.

I was in the hospital for four or five days after the surgery was complete. Although I was in severe pain, it still wasn't as painful as getting a metal bar placed under my ribcage. Besides, I had the morphine pump right by my side. However, as I began to heal, the morphine was replaced with a painkiller (also known as an opiate) called Percocet. So every four hours I would buzz the nurse for two 5 mg Percocet, as that was the timeframe and dose recommended by the doctor.

The Percocet gave me a warm feeling. It did not completely take all the pain away, but it definitely eased the pain. I remember taking Percocet while I was lying down in my hospital bed and it helped me relax. The effects of the opiate made watching television enjoyable as I became more interested and entertained by things. That fuzzy feeling of happiness made me actually look forward to my next dose of the medication. I had no idea there was any problem with taking pain medication with the doctor's supervision in a hospital setting. However, there was a suspicious way my mind was working. My thought process was beginning to alter and my way of thinking wasn't normal. Something was just off-beat. I had no clue at the time what was happening. There was a demon lurking somewhere. I didn't know when this demon would reveal itself and I certainly didn't know where, but it was somewhere feeding and growing into a tormenting creature. Deep in the shadows.

On my last day in the hospital, I was getting ready to be discharged. I asked the nurse if I could get four Percocet for the ride home, since I was going to be sitting in a vehicle for a couple hours, which would add stress on my back. The doctor said that it would be perfectly fine. On the ride home I felt that warm fuzzy feeling again. Only this time it was more intense and I soon found myself nodding off, half asleep in the backseat of my parents' vehicle.

I was given prescriptions for Percocet when I arrived home. Since I couldn't really do much of any activities in the physical sense, I spent most of my time watching television. I had to walk with a cane for the first couple months, and since it was the wintertime I was forced to walk around in my house for exercise. Percocet contributed to making my life manageable for the time being, as I was recovering from this major surgery. Now how crazy is that statement? Having opiates to manage my life in recovery? For the normal human being, only being in the post surgical condition would make that phrase comprehensible. An upcoming addict such as myself only thought it was perfectly normal. In this case we also weren't talking about the 14-year-old boy who was able to manage his life without any pain medication after having a metal rod placed under his rib cage. We're talking about Skrock, the party animal and college sophomore.

In the beginning stages of my post-operative recovery, I followed the directions labeled on the prescription bottle of my medication. I took the prescribed dose at the designated timeframe and got along fine. I still, however, loved the way Percocet made me feel. My aunt and uncle came over my house to visit me soon after my surgery. I remember taking two Percocets, and my uncle was curious how many Percocets they gave me. I just remember there were a hundred Percocets in the prescription bottle and my uncle asked "Won't he become addicted?" I thought nothing of it at the time. Hell, I was feeling good. The only problem was that the Percocet was maintaining this sense of feeling good. I was taking the medication as prescribed, I never experienced withdrawals, but I was always looking forward to my next dose of the opiate. My uncle had a point. It was a good question. But nobody really took it seriously. Especially not me.

One day while I was still on winter break, I was sitting at the computer in the living room and a thought popped into my head. I was home by myself and whether it was that I was ready to take my next recommended dose of Percocet or not, a voice out of nowhere entered the realms of my brain. The voice stated, "Why don't you try crushing the Percocet and snorting it!?" It was a controlling voice and I became intrigued with the idea. It wasn't as if I was scared to do so, but curious to experiment and find out the effects of the drug taken in this manner. I wasn't stupid. I knew that this way of taking the drug wasn't "normal." The problem was that I wasn't thinking of the effect it would have on me. I had no idea of the risk I was taking when I decided to crush up that Percocet, make a few lines, roll up a dollar bill and blow that white powder up my nostril. I thought it was the same old experimentation. A one time thing. I couldn't have been more wrong.

As the opiate traveled through my nostril and transported its way into my bloodstream, I could immediately feel the effects of the drug. It was an instantaneous feeling. It was the same warm, fuzzy feeling that I experienced when taking the drug orally, but much more powerful. So here I was, sitting at my computer after just doing my first line of Percocet, feeling on top of the world, and I have two more lines sitting in front of me. What happens next shouldn't even be questioned. And no, I didn't brush the crushed up Percocet off the desk into the trashcan.

I wouldn't say that I was off and running, but I was definitely speed walking. I loved the feeling the Percocet gave me after snorting its contents, but I wasn't doing it all the time. I wasn't trying to get caught up in that lifestyle, but every time I decided to crush a pill up, the more the drug was catching up with me.

My winter break was over and I was on my way back to UMass, accompanied by my prescribed Percocet. At this point, I wasn't taking them as prescribed, I was using them in the recreational sense. I wasn't swallowing them, I was snorting them. I was breaking the rules. I knew I would never get in trouble for snorting pills. I always made sure to do the pills by myself in my dorm room. I didn't want anyone to know my personal business. I had a single room, I lived by myself and my door was always locked in the Southwest Towers of UMass. And it was fun. Percocet was my friend. As long as I agreed to accept him into my lifestyle, we didn't have any problems.

Alcohol was another friend of mine. Whenever I drank I would also include my repertoire of snorting Percocet, which turned out to be one of the best feelings I've ever experienced. My relationship with opiates and alcohol was initiated in the Washington Tower at the Southwest section of the UMass campus. Before I headed out to drink, I would make sure to do a couple lines of Percocet. If I was just drinking by myself in my dorm room, I would have my Percocet right by my side. I didn't mind drinking by myself. My friends were still with me. Mr. Liquor and Ms. Percocet knew how to party. I dabbled with Col. Marijuana at times as well. He was awesome.

I made sure that this whole drug and alcohol relationship wasn't an everyday affair. I mean, I still had my college education at my fingertips. I didn't want to mess that up. I did so well at Franklin Pierce and I wanted to carry that same mentality to UMass. It would be a little trickier, dealing with an evolving habit, but for the most part I was on the right path. I was a smart kid. I knew I was smart kid. However, my potential was being poked at. I'm not going to lie. I studied my ass off, I did all my homework, I read all the books, I followed instructions. I really didn't slack. The only issue I had was with my Calculus class. That was the only class I ever failed. I wasn't willing to walk three miles across campus for a 9 A.M. Calculus class, being hungover half the time. So I decided that I would attempt to teach myself. The only problem was that it's impossible to teach yourself Calculus. You just can't do it. Just to give the readers an update if I'm correct, my GPAs at UMass were a 3.42 and a 2.1. The F in calculus obviously contributed to the 2.1.

UMass wasn't easy by any means. I had an undeclared major at the time, so I had a good variety of classes that I was taking. Classes were challenging, one class in particular that I remember. It was titled "The History of Africa since 1500." I remember going to the bookstore with Brendo to get my books for that class and I was dumbfounded. The class required a thick textbook, along with four or five African novels that I had to read and be tested on. Should I drop the class? I didn't, and I'm glad that I chose to take on the challenge.

For the class I had to read this book entitled "Segu." It was probably 500 pages long, and you know we have a timeframe to finish the novel and be tested on it. So here I am in my dorm room reading "Segu," taking notes literally on every page because there are about a hundred characters popping up. I'm telling you that those African novels are very tough reads. You have to really pay attention. It's funny because I remember reading those novels and it really consumes your time. I remember for literally two weeks, Brendo would call me and ask what I was up to and my response was, "Oh you know, just reading Segu!" I'm reading the novel and it takes me a couple weeks of solid reading to complete, with pages upon pages of notes. The only thing keeping me going and maintaining an interest on my behalf were the Percocets I was blowing up my nose. I really didn't know how this test was going to be, and I didn't know how to study for it. The novel was just so dense with characters, I couldn't really keep up on everything, but test day came and I just wanted to get it over with. Well, all I can remember is there were essay questions relating the novel with the textbook. I didn't read shit from the textbook. I think I received a D- on the exam. I was upset, but I looked on the bright side. I got the chance to read the most meticulous book known to man. If you asked me what the book was about today, my response would be "Haha." I ended up getting a C- in the class. I busted my ass in that class and it was the hardest C- I would ever get.

I was proud of myself. The only thing interfering with my progress was that I used prescription drugs during my studies. If that actually played a role disrupting my potential, I couldn't tell you. I was still focused on my studies, but the fact I was blowing opiates up my nose during times of study makes for a good debate. I tried to keep the sniffing out of the way of my studies the best I could. It's tough when you have access to the drug at all times. Many excuses popped in that brain of mine that determined whether I would use or not. I tried to stick with the excuses, "All of my work is done," or "It's the weekend." Other times that voice would pop into my head and say, "You deserve to take a break, just do a line and relax for a while." I was starting to get into some battles with how my mind was responding. Alcohol was beginning to creep into this battle as well. My drinking began to take off while I was indulged in my sniffing habit.

I did plenty of drinking at UMass with Brendo and Amanda, along with Nate (who was a year above us at Hoosac Valley High School) and some other friends Jared and Dave (who previously attended Wahconah Regional High School, a rival of Hoosac Valley). Like I said earlier, when I mention certain people in my story, it is not my intention to judge anyone. The people involved in my story are strictly those who were present during my trials and tribulations. So these were the main people that I hung out with while I attended UMass.

I got drunk a lot at UMass. I mean a lot. It wasn't referred to as "ZooMass" for its love of animals. It was a party school, so that's what I did. I planned to get fucked up a lot. I remember my buddies had a little birthday party for me so I began pre-gaming in my room by myself, drinking whiskey around noon. Then I went to meet up with Brendo and eventually met at Dave's dorm room. We all drank and were having a good time. I was completely hammered by the end of the night. I just kept drinking liquor, and I remember Jared walking me back to my dorm at the end of the night because I couldn't stand up on my own. I wasn't blacked out, either, because I actually remember leaning over his shoulders and walking. When I got to my dorm's entrance, I must have told the worker that I was all right to get to my room, so Jared left. From that point on I blacked out or was close to blacked out, because I don't remember much of anything. And this is coming from a guy who rarely blacks out, having a high tolerance and all. Anyways, I made it to my room somehow. I don't remember how, but I woke up the next morning in my bed, and my room was completely trashed. Tables were knocked over, food was all over the floor, drinks were spilled. It was a complete mess. I was so hungover and all I could think about was that I was responsible for creating this catastrophe. Alcohol took control of me that night. I can still picture myself stumbling into things, I mean I must have. I was sore!

I began using Percocet to help ease my hangovers. Waking up hungover is never a pleasant feeling, so snorting that Percocet when waking up in the morning was like a miracle in a sense. It got rid of the headache and calmed my stomach. It literally woke me up, too. Any opiate is considered to be a downer, but Percocet definitely lifted me up. Lifted my spirits, too. I was happy to have it. There were certain periods where I had run out of my prescription but I hadn't really developed any symptoms of withdrawal. I wasn't taking the opiates every chance I had, but I was incrementally progressing my habit. So when I didn't have Percocet, I often crushed up and snorted Tylenol. I missed the feeling that Percocet gave me, so I tried alternative ways to get that warm, fuzzy feeling back. Tylenol didn't turn out to get the job done, but I did it anyways, and I just tried to convince myself that it had some effect. It was not normal behavior by any means. Percocet was like a light switch to me. When I had the drug the light was always on and I didn't have any worries. I felt alive and connected with my surroundings. When the drug was out of the picture, the light switch was turned off. It was dark, and I was lonely.

Another good friend of mine passed away while I was at UMass. His name was Dave Shewczyk. I went to middle school with him and we became really good friends. We lost some distance and connection over the years as he moved, but we had a lot of good times as kids growing up. I remember being in my dorm room at my computer when I received a message from Pranam. He said that "Shewz" died in a snowmobile accident. How could this be happening? Tommy just passed away and now another good friend? It was a difficult time. I went to Dave's funeral with some UMass friends that all knew him as well to say goodbye. I used to lay in my bed at UMass, most of the time drunk and high, crying myself to sleep. I actually tried talking to God a lot. I was confused. I was upset. I was sad that my friends were dead.

The year was coming to an end and I was faced with another decision. Since I had an undeclared major, I would find it difficult to be able to get into a major of my choice and graduate on time. It just wouldn't work out for me and I found that it would be in my best interest to transfer to another school. I liked UMass and all, I enjoyed hanging out with my friends who went there, but I had to do what was best for me academically. I decided to transfer to the Massachusetts College of Liberal Arts in the fall of 2006, which is located in North Adams, about ten minutes away from my hometown residence. I was finally off probation from that first DUI charge that I got in high school. Since I wasn't able to find a counselor around the UMass area, like I had at Franklin Pierce, I was able to get a few counseling sessions near my hometown to finish out the terms of my probation. It was good to be free again. I didn't really learn much from my mistakes. I was still drinking, smoking pot, and snorting Percocet. I remember a few days after I got off probation, I was hanging out with some friends in our hometown of Adams. I was in my friend Nick's vehicle with a couple of other friends and we were smoking pot, parked on the side of the street. A police car slowly drove passed us, and since it was dark and the cop kept going, having to turn around, we all began to panic. Me and Jake said, "Just fucking go!" and Nick took off down the hill like a bat out of hell. We got to the bottom of the hill and took a right, speeding with no headlights in order to hide our identity the best we could. I was nervous, I mean really nervous. I just got off probation and here I am again putting myself in this horrible situation. It was like I was setting myself up for disaster all over again. Anyways, we made it to a plaza of motor homes where we hid for a while and we dodged the cops and any trouble we could have gotten into. I was so happy. I'm guessing that I probably got drunk that night. Go figure.

Towards the end of my stay at UMass, I ran out of my prescribed Percocet, and I was feeling a little lost without them. I had bought opiates when the opportunity arose, and I still loved the feelings the painkillers embraced me with. My lower back was still in severe pain and I was out of my prescribed medication. I had a CAT scan done and met with my doctor at the Boston Spine Group in Boston. It was discovered that one of the metal bolts in my lower back had loosened and my bones had begun to separate again. Another spinal fusion was scheduled for the summer of 2006. I was actually happy to be having another surgery. In my eyes, surgeries equaled Percocet, so I was looking forward to it. It's kind of sad to say. I would have said that it was bullshit at the time and that I was thinking normally. But I wasn't. I was getting off track, real quick. I was still in the driver's seat, but I was slowly beginning to lose control of the steering wheel.

So I had my surgery and it was a success. It wasn't a major task and I was able to leave the hospital the same day. I was in pain, but I had my Percocet and the summer to recover. The only problem was that I wasn't recovering. My back was recovering just fine, but I began increasing my opiate usage. It's tough when you have a prescription for over a hundred Percocets at a time that are staring you in the face. My tolerance had grown a little bit since my last experimentation with the drug, and now that I was snorting the pills for recreational use, it made the whole "take as prescribed" notion a parody. At this stage of my drug use, I began to start using by myself more often as well.

During the summer months, I was able to go outside and get exercise by walking. I had a cane that I was mandated to use. And I did. I looked like an old man, or I at least walked like one for the next month or so. I spent most of my time inside by the computer, listening to music and blowing lines of Percocet when my parents weren't home. When my parents were home,

I often got high right in my room. I had—well actually, I still have—this little desk where I had my laptop set up and I would crush my pills on it. I would crush the whole pill up, sometimes two at a time, and snort a line or two. I would then cover the remaining powder up with an ID card and put my mouse pad over that. Whenever I felt the urge to take another line, I would just uncover the entrapment and repeat. The only real area of concern was the fact that I didn't have a lock on my bedroom door. I can't believe my parents never walked in on me while I was in the act. That wouldn't have gone down well. I always kept a good ear out nonetheless. I wasn't stupid. I was a sneaky.

I remember being prescribed 180 Percocet a month a couple of times. I really didn't want to keep the prescription bottle where my parents could find it, since I was beginning to take more than the recommended dose. I began strictly snorting the narcotics and I hid them inside a winter hat in a cabinet in my bedroom. My parents began to grow suspicious, my mother especially, as I continued to go out and consistently get drunk while I was on the medication. One day I was at my friend's house for some celebration when I received a phone call from my father. He was irate as he explained that my mother had found my stash of Percocets, with too many pills missing from the prescription bottle. They also came across a pen with the ink taken out and ends cut off. They proclaimed that this could have been used as my utensil for snorting the opiates. I denied all the accusations and stated that my back was really in pain so I took more of the pills at times. I said that I had no idea what that utensil was and how it got there. When I got home I went to see if my parents confiscated my prescription drugs. The bottle was gone, along with the utensil. However, I was beginning to think like an addict before the pills were even taken. I had taken half of the pills from the prescription bottle and had another stash that was still accessible. So when I got home I went to that stash, after fighting with my parents and denying everything. I closed the door to my bedroom, made a new utensil, sat by my desk, and got high.

When my next prescriptions were filled, my mother held on to them and gave me the pills as prescribed. She would walk into my room and hand me two pills. Once she left, I closed the door and snorted both of them. Since I had no idea where my mother hid the pills, I remember calling her one time when she wasn't home and asking where they were. I was very persuasive. I didn't want to believe it at the time, but I was acting like an addict. My mother told me where they were and I took as many I could without making a noticeable dent that would attract concern. I later found all of my mother's hiding places in her room. There was a time when I was searching everywhere for my prescription. I mean hours upon hours while my parents were at work. I finally found it inside one beer stein in a cabinet of about fifty other steins. My brain would go completely nuts when searching for those prescription bottles. I kind of knew I had a problem arising. I just didn't want to think about it. These prescriptions wouldn't last forever. At least, that's what I thought.

I also began to drink heavily while I was taking Percocet. I loved to mix alcohol and opiates every chance I could. The combination of the two made the effect on my body that much more satisfying. I often drank liquor instead of beer. I mean I still drank beer, but liquor got the job done. I never really was a beer drinker. But then again, I guess you could say that I would drink anything that contained alcohol. I still had that persona that I carried on my shoulders of being that "big drinker/party animal." However, I would rather have a Perc than a drink at this point of my life. It's not like I had an unlimited supply of Percs. My prescriptions would only last me for so long. I had to start thinking outside the box.

After about a month and a half after my surgery I began to work for the Town of Adams in the Public Works department. I had worked as a seasonal worker in the past and it wasn't a bad job. I worked with my friend Jake for our four or five seasons at the job. My father Steve has been a full time worker for the Town of Adams and put in a lot of hard work to make our town what it is. His partner, Mark, and the Superintendent, Dave, have worked well together and have committed their careers to making Adams a beautiful and safe place to be. And when I say safe, I am talking about the long strenuous hours they put in to plow the roads of Adams during winter snowstorms. They also do the upkeep of local cemeteries, sporting fields, rivers, and any town-based areas. Jake and I were mainly stationed at the Bellevue Cemetery and our job basically consisted of lawn mowing and weed whacking. It was a good job to have during the summer and we had fun. The pay wasn't that great but it was good enough for a college student to get by on during his summer break.

We did our job, but we also did a lot of "dicking around." We took a lot of breaks, which pissed off some higher ups. But the way I looked at it, as long as we got the job done, they shouldn't have minded us taking a break when the sun was scorching. The real problem came when we would actually hide in the woods alongside of the cemetery and drink alcohol. We got caught by my father one time. He walked right into the woods and found us all drinking. We didn't get fired or anything, but it was definitely a stupid move. I felt awful, putting my father in that position and all.

There was a time when all of us seasonal workers, including Matt and the infamous "Striker," planned on drinking during the work day. Jake and I got a 30 pack of beer the night before and kept it in one of our vehicles. We would just fill up our mugs with beer and cut grass. The drinking started at 8 A.M. Talk about early for your first beer of the day. On the job, nonetheless! Let me tell you, by our 2:00 break we were all laying down in one of the cemetery lots—if my recollection is clear it would have been Section F or D. Maybe Dave would know. He was probably like "what are these fuckers doing!?" I think we managed to leave early that day too. Using the excuse of "It's too hot, you can dock me," perhaps. Sorry, Dave!

I can honestly say that I drank while working for the Town of Adams and I also used opiates. It's not something that I was proud of. It didn't happen all the time, but it happened. Opiates played more of a role during my employment with the town as I will talk more about later on.

During that summer working for the Town of Adams, I also ran into some trouble. Who would have thought? It was a Thursday, I was working on the banks of the Hoosic River, and it was scorching hot outside. Jake, Matt, and I were trying to make plans for after work since it was Thirsty Thursday and all. We heard about a party going on at Williams College that night, and after work we got together and decided to go.

We met up with some hometown friends who had connections to the party, and it was a good time. We were all drinking and having fun, playing beer pong and whatnot. I also decided to smoke some pot. I sometimes felt that smoking pot actually helped me drink more because it calmed my stomach down. So I drank quite a bit that night and it was getting to be time to leave. There were liquor bottles laying around this party area that were full of booze. Nobody was really claiming them so I pulled one of the most idiotic moves I'd pulled in a while that would end up biting me in the ass. For some reason, I had this empty orange juice bottle, and I decided to fill it up with booze from one of the liquor bottles.

Matt said he would drive me and Jake home, along with our friend Owen. We all piled into his vehicle and we were on our way. On the ride home, there was a man driving behind Matt that called the police because he wasn't driving like normal. This guy was actually pissing Matt off along the way, which increased the hostility on the road. Before we know it, there was a police car with its lights on behind us and Matt pulled over to the side of the road.

The police officer came over to Matt's vehicle and I went to put my hands in my pocket to hide the orange juice bottle full of liquor. The moment I put my hands in my pocket, the police officer exclaimed, "Keep your damn hands on the passenger seat where I can see them!" I obeyed his order and we were soon asked to step out of the vehicle, where we were searched. When the officer pulled the orange juice bottle out of my pocket he said, "What's in this?" In my drunken manner, I said that it was just orange juice, when clearly I knew that it wasn't. The officer opened up the container and put his nose up to the brim, smelling the contents inside. I was handcuffed and was charged with possession of an open container under 21 years of age. All of us were arrested that night and we were on our way to the North Adams Police Station. I was asked if I wanted to make a call to my parents. I was just thinking to myself, "Not again!" I decided not to call my parents; just like the other times, I wasn't able to man up to my mistakes. Jake ended up calling his parents. We all spent the night in jail and Jake's father picked both of us up in the morning. Matt and Owen found their own rides.

Jake and I also had to work in the morning. We were running late and when I walked into my house just as my father was about to leave for work, I looked at my parents with my glossy eyes. They had been worrying about me all night, so I told them, "I got busted and spent the night in jail." I mean the fact of the matter was, I couldn't really hide it. Then I saw the disappointed looks on my parents' faces and felt like a failure. I let them down again. Didn't I just get off probation? I slept for a few hours to sober up a little more and went to work for the second half of the day. Jake did too. It wasn't our decision. Our parents made us. We were back in paradise, weed whacking alongside the banks of the Hoosic River. I had the voice in my head questioning "What's going to happen to me now?"

I ended up going to court and was placed on probation for six months. I also had to pay some court fees. Jake, Owen, and I were asked to testify in Matt's trial and when the time came Jake and Owen gave their testimonies. When they came back, the judge asked them if I would have remembered anything that happened during the incident. Since Jake and Owen didn't really recall too much of anything, the court decided that another drunk witness wouldn't do much good. I didn't have to testify. I was drunk when the incident occurred, and so were Jake and Owen. It's kind of difficult to recall things that happen when you're intoxicated. My responses would have consisted of "I don't recall, sir." The judge wasted his time even talking to my friends; he should have known better!

The summer ended and I was actually off Percocet for a little while before starting my first semester at the Massachusetts College of Liberal Arts, otherwise known as MCLA. I may have bought some Percocets or Vicodin here and there, but I wasn't doing as many opiates as I had been before. I remember I had some time away from the whole opiate game before heading to MCLA. However, my back was still in severe pain and although I hadn't had any withdrawal symptoms from my previous opiate use, I still missed the feeling they gave me. I remember sitting at my house one day and that whole mentality of "thinking outside the box" came into play.

I was sitting at home by my computer one day and I told my mother that I was still in a lot of pain. I was completely off my previous prescriptions for Percocet and I didn't want to give the impression that I *wanted* the drugs but that I *needed* the drugs. I went back to thinking like an addict and became very persuasive. I was good at that. My mother believed me, and I was really in a lot of pain so I figured that it would be a good idea to call my doctor to let him know what was going on. Since I was still suffering from a lot of pain, I figured that I was entitled to more opiates. I told my doctor that I was still in a lot of pain and asked if he could send me a prescription for Percocet in the mail, since he was located in Boston. He agreed to do so, and within a couple days I had the prescription for Percocet in my mailbox waiting to be filled.

I received the prescription and I think it contained 90 pills. I wanted to keep this low key with my parents and all. I didn't want to do something stupid and give them more suspicion about my growing habit. I would make the prescription last me a while and when it was finished I had a plan that only an addict would think of. I wrote a letter to my doctor in Boston, stating that I would like a refill on my prescription medication. I just wrote what I was taking in a letter and I waited for the mail to the arrive each day. I wanted to make sure that I was the one getting the mail. I certainly didn't want my parents to stumble across a letter from my doctor in Boston. They would open it up before giving it to me. I know they would. If there was any sort of suspicion, my plan would be ruined.

I went to get the mail a few days later and there was a letter from the doctor. I was anxious to open it. It was either going to be an uplifting or devastating day for me. Well, at least that's how I was thinking. I opened it up and inside was another prescription for Percocet. I felt a sense of relief and immediately jumped into my car and went to the pharmacy. I got the prescription filled and now I could do as many Percocets as I wanted without anybody knowing my secret, especially my parents. I just had to be careful and not leave any trails leading to my prized possession. I made sure to be careful. Hell, I was the kid that was still snorting pills in his bedroom with an unlocked door. I wasn't the smartest individual at the time, but I was learning how to become a sneaky addict. At least that's what I was on my way to becoming. I was snorting pills everyday. Isn't that addict-like behavior? The fact of the matter is that it was. I had just started my junior year at the Massachusetts College of Liberal Arts and I thought I had everything under control. I actually did, as long as I had access to those circular, white pills. I could function like a normal human being and it had no influence on my abilities in the classrooms. I was a good student. I excelled in school. I was transforming into a college student who was dependent on narcotics.

My first prescription delivered through the mail had run out. I wrote another letter to the doctor to see if this system would work. Would he actually prescribe me the medication I *want* if I just ask? If I didn't exactly *need* it anymore? That's exactly what I did, and I made sure I was the one to check the mail when the prescription came in. When I wrote the letter to the doctor, I made it my duty to check the mail every day until the prescription arrived. I had to remember, there was no room for suspicious activity in this line of business. I received another prescription in the mail. I think I was getting 180 Percocets a month. At least for the two months, I believe. After that, I was getting 90 Percocets a month for a lengthy period of time. The system was working and I was getting the medication I "wanted." The tricky part was maintaining the 90 pills for 30 days. I soon found myself running out of the prescription five or six days before intended and I put myself in a hard spot. I wanted to continue to use opiates, so there were times when I had to buy them from some people I knew who also had connections to the drug.

I would make sure to write my letters a few days before the 30 day mark. That way I would be able to receive my prescription on the day it was actually scheduled to be refilled. It was always an anxious arrival when I was listening for the mailman, taking the walk down my driveway, and opening up my mailbox. I was so anxious because it was always a hit or miss. It was either a "Fuck yea!" or a "What the fuck!?" Either way, every time I opened up that mailbox, I actually prayed. I wanted that medication. When I actually came across that specific letter mixed in with the mail, it seemed as if a huge weight was lifted off my shoulders. I was happy. I was happy to have the drug. The drug I so desperately wanted.

I was doing well in school. I made sure I excelled, not to say that it was a cover up for my drug use, but I actually wanted to do good. I always had the motivation to get good grades. I wanted to set myself up for the opportunity to get a good job after I graduated. I would snort pills before class, I would snort pills after class, I would snort pills to snort pills. I was still doing all of my homework and getting great test scores. I was studying, and I was giving an honest effort. When I was at my house and all of my work was done for the night, it was "me" time. When I say "me" time, I am referring to the time where I relaxed, isolated in my bedroom, and snorted more pills. I often drank alcohol if I had any or could find any. I would usually just steal it from my parents. It was easy. Alcohol was everywhere. Liquor in the cabinet, beer in the fridge. I just had to be sneaky about what I took. If there were ten beers in the fridge, it wasn't like I took six. I would take two. If there was a half a bottle of vodka, I would fill up an empty water bottle with as much as I could without it being noticeable. I was sneaky. I wasn't even 21 years old yet and I had a growing love for opiates and alcohol. The way I looked at it, if I was getting good grades in school, then why couldn't I reward myself with these intoxicants? Most college students drink and use marijuana. Why couldn't I drink and use opiates? It was fucking prescribed, for God's sake.

I did well my first semester at MCLA. I got As and Bs. I was a good student, and I was still getting my prescriptions in the mail. Winter break arrived and I was able to hang out with some friends I hadn't seen in a while. Some of my friends were actually doing pills too, so it was a good feeling to know that I wasn't the only one. I would often share some of my pills with my friends and sometimes I would regret it. I wanted them for myself and I wanted the pills to last. But when you're drunk and you're with your friends, sometimes you turn into a generous person. I tried to keep my using a secret but it was tough when some of my friends found out that I was prescribed Percocet. My defense was to tell them how it was. In my mind I would say, "I'm prescribed this medication, and I don't have a problem. My back is in pain and I need the medication to ease the pain." It was all a bunch of bullshit, but I needed to cover my own ass. I didn't want this information to get leaked to my parents somehow. I had to make sure I was around the right people. The people I knew I could trust, who wouldn't say shit to my family.

My second semester at MCLA began and I continued with my same routine. Snorting pills and studying was like peas and carrots. It really was. I mean, it actually gave me more of an interest in my studies when I was using. It sounds kind of insane, but ask any opiate user who has just begun to grow a dependance on the drug. When you're not using you say, "I don't feel like doing this shit," and once you snort that pill you're like "All right, let's get to work!" You do your work and you can function like any other normal person. The only problem is that you begin to *need* this miracle drug to help you function. I was stepping into scary territory. However, I hadn't encountered any signs of withdrawal yet. I would wake up feeling fine. I wasn't going overboard with my pill use. On my ideal days I would try to only blow four to six pills, spread throughout the day. That was like my maximum at this time in my life. So we're talking 20 to 30 milligrams of oxycodone. Since I wasn't at the withdrawal stage yet, I tried to maintain this amount that I was using. I really tried to moderate my using, and I did for quite some time. Of course, there were days when I overdid it. Usually when I first obtained the prescription I would splurge. I mean, I had 90 Percocets sitting right in front of me. It was as if I was a fat kid and someone placed a gigantic chocolate cake in front of me. What do you think was going to happen?

I started my second semester at MCLA and it was a new and exciting upcoming year for me. I would be turning 21 years old and was looking forward to the whole life transition. You know, the stage of your life where you can actually go to a bar and drink? You could even walk into a liquor store and purchase alcohol, can you believe that? I couldn't, and I just wanted to get to that point of my life. I had spent too much time in the past few years getting in trouble with the law and finding myself on probation. Alcohol got me into a lot of trouble when I was underage, so I figured when I was finally legal to drink, I wouldn't have to worry about anything. I could buy as much booze as I wanted, drink as much as I wanted, and nobody could do a damn thing. This is coming from the same person who is still blowing lines of Percocet in his bedroom by himself every day. Yeah, don't forget about him. I thought I had everything figured out and under control. That all began to change the day I turned 21.

My grades in school were still good. I had good study habits and my drug and alcohol use never seemed to interfere with my studies. I was anxious for March 16, 2007 to come around. I wanted to be 21 years old already. Well, if you want to be precise, I was waiting for midnight on March 16th, so I could go to the bar for two hours and get hammered with my friends. I actually made this whole event thing on Facebook for my 21st birthday party, which would be held at the PNA in Adams. The PNA, also known as the Polish National Alliance, was the well known bar in Adams where most people went on the weekends. I actually remember the title of the event. It was called "Lou Bob's 21st Bombin' Bash." Lou was a family nickname that stuck with me. I really don't know how it came about, my former Uncle came up with it. My family and even some of my friends still call me Lou to this day. Not a lot of people call me Trevor. It's either Skrock or Lou. Or a trendy combination of the two. Lou Bob, Lou Bega, Skrockdiggidy, or Skrockbanger were commonplace.

It was March 15, 2007 and I was at home with my parents and my grandparents, just hanging out. I was drinking Miller High Life, trying to get a buzz on so I would be ready for the bar at midnight to celebrate my 21 years on this planet. It wasn't "Lou Bob's 21st Bombin' Bash"—that would be held the following night. So, I'm sitting at my house drinking beers, and four beers turns into eight, and eight beers turns into twelve. I guess you could say I was ready to go. My friend picks me up and I meet up with some other people at The Grille, which is another bar in Adams that people usually end up at later in the night. I was basically getting drinks, shots or whatever I wanted for free, so I got really drunk. It was awesome. I was 21 and I had the freedom to get as wasted as I wanted. I didn't care, I was 21, it was a time to celebrate.

I woke up the next morning in my bed and was pretty hungover, but I was excited. My next door neighbors known as the Sookeys (Sookey being their last name) have owned a liquor store in Adams called the Oasis for decades. Well, it's basically owned and run by Dave and Rich, the Sookey brothers. Dave is my next-door neighbor, the man of the house, and Gail is his wife. The Sookeys were like a second family to me. I grew up with their children, David, Dino, and Ramzy. I was always over at their house as a child and up until my early twenties. It was like my second home. They opened up their house to me, treated me like a son, a brother and a friend. They always took care of me. It was truly an amazing youth and adolescent life, being able to connect with such a caring and courteous family. It would take me more than a lifetime to repay them for all that they have done for me. I was blessed to have them in my life and I still am. I truly mean that with all of my heart. The door was always open and there was always Polly-O string cheese in the fridge. I think up until I was 19 or 20 years old, there would be an Easter basket full of candy with my name on it. If that isn't love, I don't know what is. Thanks, Gail!

When I woke up I decided to go to the Oasis. It was my intention to get some alcohol. I figured that if I was feeling like crap and it was my first full day being a 21-year-old, what better way to help me out then to get some booze. I didn't realize it at the time, but that is a pretty scary situation. In this newfound mind of mine, being 21 and all, I had this overwhelming ability to act irrationally. Unless you actually think that drinking straight liquor is a rational decision when you have a hangover. I'm pretty sure food and water could help out. The fact of the matter was that I was 21 years old, and I had the right to drink when I wanted to. Morning, noon, or night, it was my decision. Anyways, I got about three or four birthday nips of Goldschlager, slugged them down, and I was off to the RMV to get my new license. You know, the horizontal ones that show you're 21 years of age or older. You could tell that I just turned 21 because when they took my picture I looked like a mix between hungover as fuck and a little bit drunk. Isn't that how everybody should look the day of their 21st birthday? Probably not. Let me rephrase that. The answer is no. Not everyone in the world makes the decision to drink before they get their photo taken for their "21 and over" I.D.

After I was finished with the RMV and got my mugshot taken, I drove home and took a nap. I really needed it, considering "Lou Bob's 21st Bombin' Bash" was just around the corner. When I woke up from my nap, I got ready and went over to a friend's house to start pre-gaming. A snowstorm was in the mix for the night, so I was a little concerned about the turnout for my party. Either way, I knew my really close friends would be there. Either way, I was going to have a good time. Either way, I was going to get drunk. The Town of Adams has dealt with so many snowstorms throughout the years, so this was nothing new. I was feeling pretty buzzed and it was time to go to the PNA to party. It was time for Lou Bob to get his drink on. It was time for some shots of Goldschlager, or should I say "Lou-schlager." Line 'em up!

Since Goldschlager was my drink of choice at the time, my friends came up with the term "Louschlager," combining my nickname with my favorite drink. It was clever and everyone had fun with it. Some of my friends would call me "Louschlager," some would like to take shots of "Louschlager." It was a two way street for me. For instance, if I were to walk into a bar, someone might say, "Hey, Louschlager, do you want to take a shot of Louschlager!?" The term became a trademark for me because that's all I really drank. That's how I also got the nickname. All of my friends would always see me drinking Goldschlager, hence they put two and two together, and created a name that I would live up to. This name and trademark was not made during "Lou Bob's 21st Bombin' Bash," however. It was founded shortly after as my drinking progressed.

My 21st birthday party was a success in that I got to see a majority of my close friends and I actually wasn't too drunk. I mean, I was drunk, but not to the point where I would stumble over everything that got in my way. I actually remember everything that happened that night. My father picked me up in the town plow truck because of the snowstorm and brought me home after the party. Christ, I even remember untying my boots and putting myself in my bed with no help. If that wasn't an accomplishment in itself, then I don't know what is. I drank a lot. I guess you could say I had high tolerance. The fact of the matter was that I actually did. I was a tall, skinny kid that could hold his liquor. I was good at drinking. Just like Michael Jordan was good at basketball. You get the idea.

I was still doing well in school and during my junior year I developed a habit with alcohol. If I finished all of my work, and was happy with my effort, I would drink. I would go down to the liquor store and buy a bottle. Whether it was Goldschlager, vodka, or schnapps, it had to be liquor. No beer, no Twisted Tea, no wine. Liquor. It was easier to hide. I would tell my parents I was going to the store to get gas or scratch tickets. Then I'd come home with a bottle hidden in my jacket. I'd go into my room, shut the door, put on the television, lay down in my bed, and drink. Drink straight liquor. I would drink because I thought I deserved to. I was working hard in school. So why did I have to hide the bottle from my parents? I was legal age to drink. The answer is easy. If they ever saw me drinking straight liquor by myself, there would be a huge problem. I didn't want any problems. I wanted to drink what I wanted. It was my right to do so.

I would be laying in my bed with a bottle of Goldschlager and I would make sure that after every sip I would place the bottle under the pillow next to me. That was considered my bottle's safe spot. I didn't want it to be found if my parents walked into the room. I just wanted to relax, drink, and watch television. I mean I used to drink with parents and with my family even before I turned 21. It was sort of commonplace. It wasn't really that big of a deal if I had a few drinks at a family function. Most of my family drank, so it was acceptable under the right circumstances.

My drinking definitely progressed during my junior year, and the fact that I was drinking alone wasn't a good sign. I thought nothing of it. I was just a college student that turned 21. What do you expect? I enjoyed liquor. I liked the fact that it burned as it came down my throat and into my stomach. The effect was so much quicker. Beer wasn't even a competition.

I did well in school, and my grades were still more than satisfactory. Getting good grades was definitely a great cover up for an upcoming booze bag and pill head. I acted as if everything was fine, and I really thought it was going to be. The fact of the matter was that I was beginning to chase after something I had no intention of catching. The faster I ran, the easier it was for that something to catch me.

I was still doing pills from time to time. By the end of my junior year I was becoming dependent on the narcotics. My addiction with opiates really started to take off during the summer of 2007. I was still receiving prescription medication through the mail from my doctor in Boston and it really impacted my whole lifestyle. I was becoming dependent on those prescriptions. They were beginning to be my lifeline. I looked forward to opening my mailbox and seeing that letter from Boston. I really did. It was sickening. My parents had no idea that I was getting a prescription for Percocet. It was my secret. Well, some of my friends knew. I used to share my pills with them. I stopped, though. They were mine. Only mine. I still loved the way they made me feel. I wanted to make sure I had enough for myself. I was greedy. I was thinking like an addict.

I spent the summer working for the Town of Adams and I didn't mind it. It wasn't a difficult job, and although the pay wasn't the greatest, it was nice to work outside and get some exercise at the same time. I would begin to drink more often during the week and having access to my prescription painkillers made drinking more enjoyable. I would snort a few Percocets and swig away on whatever liquor I was drinking. The opiates intensified the effects of the alcohol. I spent a lot of time doing this by myself, if I wasn't out partying with my friends. Sometimes, I would prefer being by myself for the night. That way nobody would be able to judge me. I had that fear of being this downgraded individual because I drank a lot and did drugs. I wanted to make sure that everyone had the perception that I was a hard working student, focused on his future. I had no idea that alcohol and drugs would have any impact on my future. I thought to myself, "If I'm doing so well in school, why should I cut down on my drinking and/or drug use?" My answer was always that I was fine. I didn't have a problem. I had a grip on everything. My senior year of college was right around the corner. I'll be just fine.

The Percocets were keeping me on my feet. I was snorting pills every day and drinking a lot at the same time. My senior year at MCLA had started and I was still an ambitious student. The only problem was that I was snorting pills to help me function. I was just lost when I didn't have any pills. They were sort of my lifeline and the only thing keeping me going in school. I would wake up in the morning and snort two or three pills to start the day. I'd go to my classes, high half the time, but acting normal. It was a normal thing for me. I needed pills at all times of the day. I still did my best to conserve the prescribed monthly bottle, but it was becoming difficult as my tolerance began to climb. I went from 4-6 pills to 8-10 pills, sometimes more. I needed an alternative route to take. So I began buying Percocets or Vicodin whenever the opportunity arose. It was essential to have some sort of safety net. I needed to know that I would have opiates when I woke up in the morning. It was an aggravating feeling going to bed knowing that I had nothing to wake up to. Then the questions arise. "Where can I get some?" or "Who can I call?"

I'm not sure exactly when, but I know it was definitely during my senior year, maybe a little while before, that I began to experiment with Oxycontin. Sometimes, that was the only opiate around when I ran out of Percocets, so I said sure, why not? When you're jonesing for opiates, you'll pretty much give anything a try. I'd heard of it before and I knew it was a powerful opiate. It is considered synthetic heroin. It's basically pharmaceutical heroin that comes in tablet form. Although I don't remember the exact time I took my first line of Oxycontin, I knew that I loved it. The effect was instantaneous, so much more powerful than Percocet. You see, Oxycontin came in all forms. Based on its content of milligrams, you had your 10s, 20s, 40s, and the "Big Guy," otherwise known as 80s. I didn't really get into all the different kind of Oxys until later down the road, but you get the idea. They were expensive, a dollar per milligram. So, if I wanted an Oxy 80, I would have to pay $80.00. No joke. I didn't want to get into Oxycontin, but I also never wanted to get into Percocet, and look how that was turning out. Now this new, powerful narcotic enters into my whole realm of daily living and it's a whole new ball game. It wasn't softball either, strictly hardball.

I began working at the Berkshire Mall at a store called Steve and Barry's in October, 2007. It was that store with hundreds and hundreds different kinds of T-shirts. I didn't really mind it because it was a fairly easy job, my parents were off my back, and I was getting some extra cash. It was a tedious job, so as long as I had some opiates in my bloodstream I was good to go. The reason I bring up my job at Steve and Barry's is because I remember I had to work on Black Friday—you know, the day after Thanksgiving where everybody shops as if it's the end of the world. I had to be at work for 6 A.M. and when I woke up, I had stashed some left over Oxy 80 under my mouse pad. All crushed up and ready to go. I rolled out of bed, snorted whatever was left, maybe 20 milligrams, and I was off to work. That was one of the first vivid memories that I can remember dealing with my introduction to Oxycontin. I knew I bought it, I knew how to get it. It was just a matter of if it was actually around, and if I had the money to purchase it. I always had my prescription opiates on the back burner, but it was still only a limited supply.

One morning, I arrived to work late. I had to work at 9 and the pharmacy wasn't open until then. The fact that I had to get my prescription before work wasn't even a question. Once I got the Percocets, I went home, blew a few up my nose, and went to work. I arrived to work around 10 and made an excuse that I overslept or some shit. What did I care anyway? This wasn't my fucking dream job.

The job wasn't really holding up as the business was beginning to struggle. I wasn't getting nearly enough hours for a somewhat decent paycheck and my thoughts towards sticking around were dwindling. I remember I was driving to work one morning and a voice in my head said, "Why the hell are you even going to that stupid job today?" I thought to myself, "Yeah, for real, is it even worth it?" I pulled my vehicle to the side of the road, called work, and told them that I was sick. I said I wouldn't be coming to work today. Since my parents were home, I couldn't go home and be like "Yeah, I just got sick on the ride to work and called out." I had to come up with a plan. I ended up driving to one of the back roads in Adams, parked the car and began blowing lines of Percocet. I am almost positive that I also started to drink. It wasn't even noon yet. If I'm not mistaken, my parents were leaving town that day so I had to wait for them to leave to actually be safe to walk into my house. Dodging work to drink and blow pills, waiting for my parents to leave town. How pathetic. I ended up quitting the job in March 2008.

There were a few people I knew that had connections to get opiates. It wasn't ever guaranteed, but if I was out of stock, I at least had some numbers to dial. I hated to come across as that guy who actually starts buying opiates, but the more I used, the more I needed them. If I woke up in the morning, and I didn't have any opiates, I wouldn't feel good. I felt nauseous. My muscles were tight. I wouldn't have any energy. It sucked and I knew that it wasn't a good sign. I was an addict. I was probably an addict when I was at UMass. Hell, I was probably an addict the moment I was laying in my hospital bed anxiously awaiting my next dose. I had been using and abusing the pills for quite some time. They had caught me. Now Oxycontin was in the picture and it wasn't a joke anymore. That voice inside my head began whispering, "You're in trouble." I knew it, but I didn't want to believe it. If I was out of pills, I would use my skills. Not my coping skills to turn away from the drug, I didn't have any of those. I used what skills I had to to encounter them, to get my next fix. I would contact people. I always seemed to manage to find pills. I was a happy camper when I found that hook-up. When I actually found a way to get more when I was completely out, a huge weight was lifted off my shoulders and I felt a sense of relief. I would jump into my car and my blood began flowing with eagerness as I was on my way to purchase the pills. I always seemed to have money when it came time to buy pills. I mean if I didn't have enough cash on me, I always had some money saved if needed. It was the start of a hellish lifestyle. I tried to stick with Percocets or Vicodin. They were cheaper. Oxycontin, on the other hand, was just outrageous.

At that point of my life, I would rather have spent $80.00 to get 16 Percocets rather than one Oxycontin. I figured I could make 16 Percocets last for two days, maybe even three. One

Oxycontin pill might be gone in one. I really tried to rationalize the two forms of opiates, but when it came down to it, Oxycontin was beginning to show its face more and more. I just needed to focus on college, which was coming into the realms of completion. It's not easy juggling opiates with college. It's really not. It's a daily task. A daily struggle.

Since I was in my final year of college, looking to graduate with a Bachelor's Degree in Business Administration with a concentration in Sports Management, I really needed to be able to put that on the top of my list. I didn't want opiates to control any aspect of me, or my degree. I really didn't come across any serious problems. I mean there were times like I said before where I needed pills, but I always managed to track them down. I was putting my prescription narcotics all up my nose about a week earlier than recommended, so being able to purchase opiates on the side was necessary. I always seemed to find a way, and my schooling was uninterrupted. However, there was this sort of "bump" that occurred towards the end of my final semester. Well, I guess you could say this bump was double the size of ordinary bumps. Fuck it, it was triple the size.

I was doing excellently in school, but I began to have some meetings with advisers of MCLA because there were certain classes I needed to take in order to graduate on time with my classmates. I guess I wasn't really following the requirements, such as core classes and such, and I was off in that sense. I really didn't want this happening. Not now. I just didn't want my parents to have to deal with it. They had this huge graduation party planned for me already and everything. The invitations were already sent. Now I had this shit to deal with. I made efforts on my behalf to do anything I could to be able to graduate on time, but it was no use. The only option I had was to take the classes I needed, along with an internship, over the summer months, and receive my diploma in August of 2008. I pleaded my case, and I was at least allowed to walk with my classmates in May. I just wouldn't have my degree in order until

August. Was it a big deal? Not really. But telling my parents was going to be tough. I had enough on my table with these fucking opiates.

The past few months, my doctor had lowered the number of Percocets that he was giving me during a month's time. I went from 180 to 90 to 60. It wasn't the best situation in the world, but at least I was still getting something. I was always able to find more if I needed to. So, I'm working for the Town of Adams while I just finished up my supposed last semester at MCLA. Before I go to work, I talk to my mother on the computer while I'm on my lunch break. I think I snorted the last Percocet from my prescription and told her of my school situation. She said that we would talk when we were both home from working.

When I got home from work, there was disappointment in my mother's eyes. The disappointment had nothing to do with my schooling situation, rather my secret of drug addiction. Since I had been receiving letters in the mail from my doctor in Boston, I had to think of a way to cover up the evidence. The most logical way would be to throw away the envelopes in a dumpster outside the location of my residence, but of course my mind wasn't in a "logical" state. I would end up hiding each individual envelope in one of my college textbooks. Each envelope, scattered in between separate pages of the book, was located inside my backpack, along with numerous other books. It was a perfect hiding place. I thought it was, anyways. I mean, why would my mother be snooping in my room, looking inside my backpack, when I wasn't home? Did I have something to hide? I thought she wouldn't have a clue about anything. However, my mother had always been concerned with my past behavior involving drugs and alcohol. I knew she was. She had expressed it before. I thought it was a phase, but it wasn't. She obviously had suspected something was up. She sensed it and she knew exactly where to go. Inside my room, where I isolate myself, she would find a sign, a clue. That's exactly what she did, and I had no idea it was coming. The disappointment and fear in her eyes was impossible not to notice. My father would have never checked inside my room. He wasn't like that. He respected my privacy and was more pissed off at my doctor for doing what he did.

So here I am, put on the hot seat, all attention on me and all I have to say is "What? I was taking them for my pain. I don't have a problem." I was going through withdrawals through this whole scenario, which made the debate for my concerned parents a lost cause. I was in the denial stage and did everything in my addicted state of mind to persuade them that I was all right. I was so sick, though. I remember that day pretty well. I had no pills, my parents were all over me, and all I could think about was, "Where can I find some pills?" My father brought me to meet some family friends at the Little League baseball field in Adams, also known as Beaver Bard Park, where I played as a kid. He had to sign something for his friend or something and I was sitting there in the stands watching these kids play baseball, enjoying themselves. Their proud parents, family members, and friends in the crowd cheering them on. And I'm just sitting there, withdrawing from opiates, thinking to myself, "How the hell did I get here?" It was such a depressing day. My father ranting about the "Fucking stupid college advisors," and "The fucking idiotic doctor." I just wanted to get high. I needed to feel better, and everything going on around me wasn't helping. Nothing would be better until I had that certain pill crushed up, ready to go up my nose. I was sick. I knew I was sick, but I didn't want to get better. I just wanted to feel better.

I finished my classes at MCLA during the spring and would have to take a couple courses over the summer in order to receive my bachelor's degree. I also would get the opportunity to take an internship for the North Adams SteepleCats collegiate baseball team. I interviewed for the internship position and was now a part of a sport's organization. Although my graduation hadn't gone as planned, I was still able to walk with my classmates in May and have my graduation party that same day. Just having a couple classes to take during the summer, and now having this internship, I guess you could say things were looking up. My family thought I was doing well, but I was still an addict. I was drinking a lot, too. Drinking a lot more than your average college student. Drinking a lot more by myself. Pills and booze were still controlling me as I tried to steer into the right lane. I needed to get that bachelor's degree. I needed to prove to myself, and more importantly to my family, that I wasn't a failure. I wanted to get that high paying job. I wanted to do something I loved. It was just so damn hard too get into that right lane. It was even harder to stay in that right lane. Blockades of pills and booze tend to make it difficult.

I met with my doctor in Boston, and with my parents' concern, he was forced to take me off the prescription painkillers. I departed with a final prescription of 30 Vicodin and said my final goodbye to that doctor. I said to myself, "Thanks a lot, Doc. I've been taking large quantities of Percocet for the past year and a half and you think you can fix me with 30 Vicodin? What a joke." I didn't know how the hell I was going to get through this stage of my life, I only knew it was going to get worse. Without the guidance of prescription medication, I turned to the "Big Guy," Oxycontin for answers. I had nowhere else to go. Oxycontin had me at hello. I was completely addicted to Oxycontin shortly after those envelopes stopped being delivered to my mailbox. The next seven months would be one of the toughest struggles I ever had to go through. Having a bar in my chest was like getting stung by a bee compared to the horrific lifestyle of my Oxycontin addiction. I wasn't Trevor Skrocki anymore. I was a liar. I was a thief. I was an addict.

Part II: The Road to Recovery

It was May 2008, and the day of graduation. I was getting ready to head down to MCLA, but before I went, I blew an Oxy. I wouldn't be able to handle this big event without being high. I wouldn't be able to handle it going through withdrawals. I walked with my classmates, and when my name "Trevor Skrocki" was called, I walked up and shook hands with the president of MCLA, high on opiates. When the ceremony was over, I went home and had what was left of my Oxycontin. After that, it was time to drink. There were two kegs of beer and plenty of liquor. I knew I had a problem that was growing, but I was happy. Didn't I have a reason to celebrate?

We integrated my graduation party with my father's 50th birthday party, so plenty of family and friends joined for the special occasions. Every now and then I would step away from the party and go into my room, where I would blow whatever opiates I had. Later on in the night, a lot of my friends started showing up and it was getting to the point where "anything goes." A lot of my family was intoxicated and doing their own thing. I, on the other hand, had friends in my room with the door closed, snorting pills. I don't usually take the Lord's name in vain, but Jesus Christ. What if someone had walked in? What if one of my little cousins opened that door? The fact of the matter was that I didn't really give a shit back then. I was so caught up in getting high and drinking that *what ifs* really didn't phase me. I didn't get caught up in the whole realm of consequences. I was completely oblivious to how to live a healthy and normal life. I was sick, and the sad part was that I had to keep it a secret. I didn't want to play the whole denial game. I could tell you it's an easy game to play, but it brings heartache to your family. It's just a game I'd rather stay away from. For now, at least.

I woke up the next morning looking to help my hangover with the couple lines of Percocet I had left over. I think I bought some off one of my friends at the party. Anyways, I blew one or two Percocets, and it was time to open my gifts. The gifts I received mainly consisted of money, which was all right with me. While I was opening each card, not really reading its contents, but seeing how much money people stuffed in each one, I wondered where I was going to buy some opiates. I was all out, and I needed more.

When I finished opening my gifts, I called one of my connections to see if there were any pills I could buy. It turned out there was Percocet 10 mg for $10.00 a piece. I took $200.00 out of recently opened graduation cards and told my parents I was going to get a coffee or something in that nature. Going to get a coffee was one of my well known cover-ups when leaving the house to get opiates. I left and returned with 20 Percocets, thinking all of my problems were solved for the day. Shortly after, my mother throws the suspicion card in my face. She counted all of my money before I left to get "coffee" and when I returned, she recounted the total amount and realized $200.00 was missing. She called me out on it and I strictly stated that the money was mine. She had no authority over it. I left it at that and turned on the denial switch in the humiliated brain of mine. I became good at dissolving conflicts by using denial tactics. "What did you do with the money?" she asked. My response, "Nothing, I just wanted to keep some for myself if I need it." I kept confrontations like this as simple and understandable as possible, even if the suspicion level was reading at a high level. Didn't I have the right to have some control of my money that was given to me for my efforts throughout college? I did bust my ass. I didn't make the Dean's List three times by slacking off. I was able to excel, even through drug and alcohol abuse. Nobody ever really knew about that but myself. I wished it could stay like that. Unfortunately, it can't. It's the truth, and people really need to know the struggle I was going through. They don't need to understand, but my friends and family deserve to know.

I spent the next several months battling with opiate addiction. I was a full blown addict and now, not only did I have to work for the Town of Adams, but I also had to complete my summer courses along with my internship with the North Adams SteepleCats. My relationship with alcohol was still intact, but opiates were a necessity. It seemed whenever I was high on pills, it was likely that I would be drunk as well. The two went hand in hand. When I snorted that line, it was as if I became a moth. A light would turn on and I would drink. Get the idea?

I really didn't *need* alcohol, I preferred opiates. Alcohol just stepped in from time time, mainly at nighttime when I was alone in my room. If it wasn't there, no big deal. I needed opiates. If I didn't have them, I would have withdrawals. It would only take 6-12 hours for withdrawals to set in, depending how much of the drug I was taking. Withdrawals were no laughing matter. They sucked. Unspeakable physical and psychological pain. In most cases, intolerable. I wasn't able to eat or sleep. I found it difficult to even hold any liquids down. I would often vomit. I was hot. I was cold. I was shaking. I felt like I was trying to crawl out of my own skin. Nasty, nasty pain. I don't wish it upon anyone. I would try to drink alcohol when I went through withdrawals, and that wasn't the easiest thing to do. Although it eased some of the pain, I often found myself vomiting. I couldn't hold the liquor down. I was drinking too much when I was high. My body couldn't handle it. I needed opiates. They were the only thing that could make me feel normal. They were the only thing that could help me function.

The summer had come along and I began my summer courses. I wasn't that worried about the classes, I was more worried about having a continuous supply of opiates. I completed and passed my final courses at MCLA. I also completed my summer internship with the North Adams

SteepleCats. It wasn't easy and there were days when I felt as if I were on the edge of failure, but I made it through. There were some dark days, though. There were some rough, agonizing days.

I remember being out of opiates, going through withdrawals, just trying to find a way to get money. I had no money, and I had no pills. I had a problem. Crawling in my skin, digging through shoe boxes in my parents' bedroom, looking for money. I needed that fix. I would look everywhere in their bedroom. Under the bed, under the mattress, in dresser drawers, anywhere and everywhere I would rummage my way through, looking for the only thing that could help me get opiates ... Money. I was going so insane that I would backtrack through shoe boxes just to make sure I didn't miss anything. I was so desperate. I was in a lonely and dark place. I wasn't Trevor Skrocki the outstanding basketball player anymore. I was Trevor Skrocki the drug addict. I wouldn't have said it at the time, but I had to be an alcoholic. I had to. I drank a lot too. There's no denying that.

One day, as I was on a routine search for money in my parents' bedroom, I came across a shoebox on the top shelf of the closet. I opened it up and found a black box inside. I took it out and opened it up. There were hundreds and hundreds of dollars inside. Straight cash. There was also a piece of paper that had the amount of money written down inside the box as well. There was a couple thousand dollars. I felt like I hit the jackpot. I was so excited, I could begin to feel my blood rush with such velocity that I could practically sense being high on opiates. I had to be careful how much I took. I didn't want it to be obvious, so I just took like $100.00 for the time being. That way I could at least buy an Oxycontin 80 mg and think about future moves.

I ended up taking an extra $200.00 or so and one day was questioned by my mother. She asked if I had taken any money from her room and I said that I hadn't. I told her she probably forgot to write down the current amount when she took some money out last time. I was in denial. I knew how to play that whole denial pretty well. I was actually getting pretty good at it. It wasn't like I was going to say "Yeah, Mom, I took $300.00 from you because I'm a drug addict." It doesn't work that way. I needed to make sure I covered up my tracks well. This being my first actual big theft and all, I kept it moderate. If there were, let's say, $1,000.00 missing, the suspicion quite possibly could have been all over me. I didn't really have a great track record with being honest to my parents. I may have gotten off the hook this time, but I did not want any more questions asked. I had to be a little smarter next time. I knew for a fact that this wouldn't be the last time I would steal from my parents.

During my internship with the North Adams SteepleCats, I would bring a bottle of liquor and keep it in my car. My main priorities consisted of bringing ice to the field, assembling event equipment, and organize some activities for the children. I had the freedom to roam out to the parking lot and swig my bottle of "Louschlager," whenever I felt entitled to do so. Hey, it made the game much more exciting if I had a hefty buzz on. It got to the point where I began pouring liquor into my thermos and walking around the stadium as if nothing was wrong. It got to the point where my supervisor said that he heard from another staff member that I was drinking on the job. I'm sure he could have smelled the alcohol on my breath. I'm sure he wasn't the only one who could. He wanted me to stop my irresponsible actions.

There was a time when I left the stadium, numerous times, to pick up opiates or just kill some time in general. One of my superiors caught on to the fact that I was randomly leaving for no reason at all. It was brought to my attention and I was given a warning. I didn't want to lose the opportunity to receive my bachelor's degree in August. Not this close to the end. I had to be careful. I was lucky. I was granted a second chance and completed the internship with no further signs of suspicion. I made sure to drink in the parking lot and pick up opiates after the game was over.

August arrived, and I received my diploma. I officially received my bachelor's in Business Administration, and it didn't really matter. I was so addicted, I couldn't have cared less. I was still working for the Town of Adams. I had been during the summer as well, while interning for the SteepleCats and taking classes as well. While working for the Town of Adams, I had been working by myself, taking care of the public ball parks. I would load up my car with whatever equipment I needed for the day and I was off on my own. I would often go into the public restrooms located on the ball fields and snort Oxycontin. If I didn't have opiates, I couldn't work. If I was having withdrawals, I would hide in the woods and force some liquor down my throat, praying I could contact someone who had access to opiates. I didn't have all the money in the world, so I began tapping into my savings account. There was money in there. Hell, all my graduation money was locked and put away in my savings. All I needed was to find where the hell I put my bank book, and everything would be all right. When I found it, I began withdrawing money to keep away my own physical withdrawals.

My parents became more and more suspicious as I refused to allow them access to my bank account. I said that it was my money and they had no authority over it. I was a grown man, and I had the right to what was mine. There was no possible way that I would give them my bank book. My money was my lifeline, but it wouldn't last forever.

I began stealing from my grandparents when the opportunity presented itself. When I was at their house one day for a family function, I decided to go into their bedroom when everybody else what outside. I opened up a box on the top of the dresser and their were a few $100.00 bills. I took one and I would do that from time to time. I wanted to be sneaky and leave little suspicion. It was part of my whole game plan. I was stealing from my family and I wanted to hurt them as little as possible. I didn't want them to know I was deceiving them. I couldn't help what I was doing. I wish I could, but I really couldn't. It was sad.

My grandmother, my Babci, had a major surgery done over the summer and she was prescribed Percocet for pain. One day I'm visiting her at her house with some family and I spot the bottle of pills on the counter in the kitchen. A huge trigger sets off in my brain. All I can think is that I need some of those pills and I need them now. Family is scattered around, some only a few steps away from me. My Babci is resting in the living room a few feet away from where I am standing. When the time is right, I grab the bottle of pills and dart into the bathroom. I open the bottle and take about ten pills. I don't want to make it obvious. I want to steer away from suspicion, so I take about ten since there are maybe eighty pills altogether. I retreated from the bathroom, sneakily placing the bottle of pills into their exact location, without a single family member seeing me. I was one sneaky addict. I took chances, I took risks, just to get those stupid pills. I couldn't help it. Temptation is a hard thing to steer away from. If you put a bottle of pills in front of a drug addict, he's bound to risk everything to get it. That's how I was. I didn't care about anything. I was stealing Percocet from my ailing grandmother, for God's Sake. I certainly didn't give a shit about her. Well, I did, but that was no way to show it. I was really, really sick. I wasn't Trevor Skrocki the baseball pitcher. I was Trevor Skrocki the drug addict.

It wasn't the last time I would steal from my grandparents either. I stole more money. I stole more pills. I remember one day I actually went looking through my Babci's purse for pills. I found them and stole them. There were times when I was in desperate need for money. One day, when my grandparents were not home, I went inside their house and took some keys to brake into a few of my aunts' homes. I always made sure I planned these events accordingly. I made sure nobody was home and wouldn't be when I arrived or left. I don't think I found any money, but I looked. If it was there, I would have taken it. I was going to all lengths to steal from my family. I was hurting those closest to me. All I cared about was myself.

I usually had some good connections when I needed to buy opiates. I would buy in bulk, too. I wouldn't just buy one or two. I would spend $300.00 to $400.00 at a time on opiates, mainly Oxycontin. I found ways to steal and became good at it. I used to drive a buddy of mine down to a nursing home where he knew someone that was selling Oxycontin, and I'd just park and wait. I'd leave with a bunch of Oxycontin 40 mg, snort one while driving and head back to town. Just like that. I did it every month for a while.

I used to drive around with Oxycontin on me all the time. I remember I had this little setup. You see, I would put all of my pills inside one of those candy mint dispensers. I would put that inside a silk case for sunglasses, along with my snorting utensil (a pen that was cut from both sides), cards (such as ID cards, used to dice and make straight lines for snorting), and most importantly, a hose clamp used to grate Oxycontin pills. Before snorting any Oxycontin pill, one must first get the coating off the pill. The easiest way to do that, the way I did it, was I simply put the pill in my mouth to moisten it. From there, I just used a paper towel or something of that sort to completely wipe off and diminish the coating from the pill. So if I was getting ready to blow an Oxycontin 80, it wouldn't be green anymore. It would be white. The reason for removing the coating was to get rid of the time release. That way, when you snort it, the effects are much more powerful and instantaneous.

It was risky business driving around with my supply on me all the time. If I ever got pulled over and caught with my stash on me, I could have gone to jail for a long time. That conception never really impacted my decision-making, and I figured that I was a safe driver. It would never happen to me. I could be pulled over or parked somewhere, in a parking lot, wherever and be snorting Oxycontin. Couldn't I get busted doing that? I thought nothing of it. Whenever I snorted pills in my car, I made sure nobody was looking. I never wanted anyone to witness that. I tried to make sure I was in a secure location, such as my locked bathroom, to do the sniffing. If I did it at my house, I made sure my parents weren't home. It's kind of funny, though, although I didn't have a problem snorting Percocet in my bedroom with my parents home, I found it against the law to snort Oxycontin. It's like Oxycontin was this hardcore drug that you really didn't want your family to find out you were doing. That's exactly right, in a sense. You wouldn't want your parents to find out you were using heroin, would you? That's why most addicts would shoot up in the bathroom, where nobody could see. Oxycontin is actually considered as pharmaceutical heroin. Although I never used heroin, or thought about using needles, I was still addicted to a heroin-based drug. Most people don't know that.

On the hunt for money, and the need for Oxycontin, I became a sick thief. I would go down to the Oasis liquor store and hang out in the back room. As I stated before, the Sookeys owned this business, and they were my second family. I began stealing money from them. Right out of the desk of their family-run business. I couldn't help myself. I opened a drawer one day when I was in the room by myself and there happened to be money inside. If the drawers were locked, I found a key to unlock them. I stole, and I stole, and I stole. I was a sick drug addict, stealing from my second family who always had their door open for me. A family that was good to me. A family that loved me. And I turned my back on them. I feel ashamed. I feel regret. I can't take back my actions. It sucks. Back then I would do anything for that pill. I would go to any lengths to feed my drug addiction. It's such a wretched lifestyle. Living day by day for a green little fucking pill. A green little fucking pill that costs $80.00. I would have never thought my life was coming to this, but I felt trapped. I felt like I had nowhere to go. No one to talk to. All by myself, in my mixed up brain, searching for survival in one little green fucking pill. That's all I knew. It's all I knew.

I found a connection that was able to get me Oxycontin anytime I wanted. Anytime, all I had to do was call. It gave me a sense of relief knowing I could get this drug whenever I wanted. I was blowing Oxycontin on a day to day basis. Through the fall of 2008 I was snorting 80-120 mg of Oxycontin a day. Sometimes less, but that was probably the best average I can come up with. Summer months fluctuated, but let's just say I was snorting Oxycontin on a regular basis for over a year. It was an everyday need now. And I needed a lot of it. My tolerance just fucking skyrocketed. If I didn't have the pill, complete, utter withdrawals set in. It was a viscous nightmare that I was living. The longest I went without the pill when I became addicted was two days. The longest two days of my entire life. Each second was the longest second. It's crazy how much time plays a role when you're laying in your bed, unable to fall asleep, wishing time would speed up. All you can do is lay there in complete disarray, praying to God you can fall asleep. You pray and you pray and you pray. When nothing happens, you give up and blame God. It's an awful, disheartening cycle. I remember I used to pinch my arms and bite my lips. Anything to keep my mind off the withdrawals. Forget watching television, the only thing on your mind is that little green fucking pill.

After going through such a painful, lengthy withdrawal, I was able to track down some money and buy some Oxy. I was happy again. Thankful again. Thankful that I wasn't in any more pain. I began to wrap around the idea that this addiction was going to be an everyday struggle, but every time I was able to get Oxy and feel better, I figured everything would be all right. Everything would turn out just fine. I wanted to believe that. I tried to believe it. But I knew it wasn't true. I knew I was in trouble and the only way to keep my mind away from that trouble was getting high. I didn't want to surrender. I had no idea what that even meant. I never surrendered in sports. Why would I surrender to this piece of shit that was destroying my life? Not a fucking chance. If I wanted to beat this addiction it was going to be by myself. I didn't need anybody's help. The more I used, the more I actually felt this way. It really began to scare me.

One day, I'm sitting at my house. No pills, no money. As I'm fighting through withdrawals, I begin searching for money around my house. I'm looking everywhere and finally open up a filing cabinet in the spare room. I'm really looking through this cabinet, even though it seemed as if the only thing inside were files. I pull through all of the files, all the way to the back. I come across a black box. The same black box that I found before in the shoe box on the top shelf of my parents' closet. I open it up and look inside. There is a lot of money, a couple thousand I would say. At least over a thousand dollars. "I'll just take some and repay them," I thought. I figured if I stole from my parents I would be able to find a way to steal from someone else to pay them back. How sick is that? So I end up taking a couple hundred and buy some Oxycontin. A few days later, I run out of pills and money, so I take another couple hundred. A few days later, the same exact thing happens. I think I end up taking $700.00 and never put a penny back. Did I really think that they weren't going to notice? I was just hoping they weren't going to go inside that filing cabinet for a while. I mean a long while. Things went unnoticed. For a while at least.

Deep in my addiction it is Christmas Eve of 2008. I'm out of Oxycontin and am going through withdrawals. I have to go down to the Oasis to pick up some grab bag gifts for the evening where my family will meet at my grandparents' house. Although I don't have any money, I don't plan on stealing any. It is Christmas Eve, and I knew there wouldn't be a chance to. I wasn't allowed in the back room anymore. I knew there was suspicion pointed in my direction. I got the grab bags and was on my way back to my house. While in my car, I begin to vomit out the window as I'm driving back home. I'm in a bad state of mind and need an Oxy. I call my connection and he isn't around until later. I have no money and my parents are leaving to go up to my grandparents' house. I tell them I will meet them there. I have to get this situation under control before I even think about spending Christmas Eve with my family.

I finally persuade my connection to spot me an Oxy and say that I will pay him back the next day, which would be Christmas Day. Once I get the pill, I snort about 20 mg and head up my Babci's. I have some drinks, and then Christmas Eve dinner with the family. Before we begin to open presents, I make a trip to the bathroom where I snort another 20 mg. I plan on saving the final 40 mg for Christmas Day. It's really all that I'm going to have. I was hoping to get some money from relatives, but I don't. I'm in trouble. My connection calls me and says that he needs the money tomorrow. I say that I will get it to him even though I have nothing. I just kept drinking with the family and try to keep my mind off the whole situation. It was Christmas Eve. I didn't want to have to worry about this shit. I wasn't Trevor Skrocki the superb soccer goalie. I was Trevor Skrocki the drug addict, trying to get by on Christmas Eve with his family.

I wake up on Christmas Day feeling hungover and in dire need of Oxycontin. I run downstairs to the bathroom and crush up the remainder of the pill and blow it right up my nose. I don't have any money, I can't pay my dealer, and don't know what I'm going to do. I open presents and have dinner with some of my family. Before I attempt to eat, I am sitting at the table and begin to feel sick. I actually need more opiates, my tolerance has just gotten so high. I run to the downstairs bathroom and vomit in the toilet, making sure nobody notices what I'm doing. I come back to dinner and force down a little bit of food. This Christmas Day isn't turning out to be what I expected. I just didn't want to ruin it for my family. Not today, I thought. Not on Christmas.

My parents and my grandparents left my house to go to my aunt's and I decided that I would just stay home to watch the basketball game. However, I had a different plan on my agenda. Since I knew my grandparents weren't going to be home, I drove up the street to their house, and since I knew where their key was, it was easy access to the inside. I began searching for money, pills, anything really. I needed something to keep me afloat. I was beginning to sink and I couldn't stand going through withdrawals on Christmas Day. I didn't want to have to struggle, I wanted to feel better. To end that struggle, the only way I knew how to feel better, to stay afloat, was to steal. I was a thief, I knew I was, but that whole mentality of feeling sorry for yourself goes out the window. I didn't care, I was sick, and I would do anything to get my next fix. Stealing from my family may be a hard thing to do, at first I thought it was, but when the disease controls your actions and your ability to think rationally, everything goes out the window. I had one thing to do. One job. I had to get opiates. I had to get money. Somehow, some way. It had to be done. If that means stealing from my loving family, then so be it. I only cared about myself. I wanted to stay afloat.

While searching in my grandparents' house, my main focus was to find money. I couldn't find any. I looked everywhere. I had stolen from them in the past. Maybe they tightened up their security. I figured that was the case. There had to be some pills at least, I thought. I had stolen pills in the past from my grandmother. Maybe she tightened up the security on the pills as well. I felt as if I'd lost the whole game. The whole scheme of my plan was out of my control. I was in a lonely, dark place. Nobody really knew the pain I was going through. That's the scary part. Being all alone in your addiction. Nowhere to go. Nowhere to turn. I just had this torturous demon lurking over me, laughing at me when I was struggling. This demon knew I was in trouble and all it asked is that I stay on the same road I have been on. The road of addiction. It wanted to see me suffer. It wanted to see the addiction take control of me. It had. The demon wanted to see me die.

Asking for a sign of possibility was my main concern. I

needed opiates and I kept searching. I went through one of the dresser drawers and found a prescription bottle. It was my grandfather's Vicodin, and some weight lifted off my shoulders. I would be able to take just enough to make it semi-unnoticeable, and still feel semi-good. Vicodin isn't going to get me super high or anything, but at least I wouldn't have to worry about any withdrawals. I popped about six Vicodin in my mouth and went back to my house. I went inside my bedroom, closed the door, and drank a bottle of Sambuca. I needed to forget that I had nothing for tomorrow. You know that song "No shoes, No shirt, No problems?" Well, when I woke up in the morning, I would have no pills, and no money. Now that would be a problem.

I began to have a bad feeling the night I went to bed on December 25, 2008. I knew my parents were going to the casino the next day and I knew I stole all that money from the filing cabinet, never putting it back, not a cent. I felt nervous about the whole situation. I figured that they would be taking some of that money to the casino, but at the same time I was praying that they weren't. I woke up on December 26, 2008 early in the morning, engulfed in withdrawals. Laying in my bed, my bones aching, my body shaking, wanting to just crawl out of my skin, I heard my parents getting ready. I just wanted to hear the house door shut and see the car drive away. I wanted to avoid the problem, but then I heard the filing cabinet open. I knew I was in trouble. I knew something was going to happen. Something I couldn't steer away from.

My mother told my father that money was missing. A lot of money was missing. At least $700.00 was missing. Money that I stole. Money that I knew I stole. But I was in denial. Denial is such a powerful mechanism of addiction. It actually begins to control your human nature. I didn't want to surrender. I was scared to. I was scared of the future. Scared of the future without opiates, which were my lifeline, my enemy, and my friend.

Questioning began to form and my mother began to point the finger at me. I knew that I was the main suspect so when she asked if I took the money, denial came veering in with a full head of steam. I denied that I took any money. When my parents asked me for my bankbook, I told them that they had no right to see it. I was in denial, and I also knew that I had no money left in my bank account. All of the money was gone. All of my graduation money was gone. I spent it all on drugs and alcohol, mainly drugs. I spent nearly $2,000, my total savings, on opiates. There was also the money that I stole that went to drugs and alcohol. I couldn't tell you how much I stole, but it definitely was in the thousands. Thousands of dollars that I stole to keep my addiction alive. If I had to estimate, I probably spent nearly $10,000 on opiates in five months.

The confrontation got heated and my parents knew something was up with me. They told me to either confess or get the fuck out of the house. I was in such denial that I got out of my bed and said fuck it. I walked right out the door with my keys and started my car in the freezing cold. I remember my windshield was completely frozen and I was just sitting inside my car, waiting for it to warm up. My mind was all over the place, I was really stuck and I couldn't figure out what my next move was. So I just sat inside my car, waiting. Waiting for something to happen, contemplating what my next move would be.

A few minutes go by and my father comes outside. He opens up the door of my car and tells me to come back inside the house. Instead of driving away, something in my head clicks and basically forces me to turn off the ignition. I walk back inside my house without a clue, dumbfounded about this whole situation. The only thing I know to do is to go back into my room. The room where I isolate. I lay down on my bed and begin to watch television as my parents pace back and forth around the house. I'm having withdrawals, stuck outside my comfort zone, struggling with reality. A few moments later, my mother walks into my room and sits down by my bedside. She caresses my foot with her hand and asks me in a quiet, but concerned voice, "Do you have a problem?" It was like a beam of light came down from above and graced me with comfort. I couldn't lie anymore. I just couldn't. I had no more fight left in me. I was exhausted. For the first time in two years I was honest. Not only with my parents, but with myself. I told my mother straight forward that I was addicted to Oxycontin as tears rolled down my cheeks. It was one of the toughest things I've ever had to do, but I am so grateful that my mother had the audacity to approach me in the manner that she had. If it wasn't for her, I don't know what would've happened. I finally admitted that I had a problem, and it felt good. It felt like I had a chance to get well. At the same time, I really didn't know what to expect. I was scared. Scared, but willing.

My parents decided to call the local detox facility, also known as the McGee Unit, to see if they had an open bed for me. It turned out that they would be able to take me in that same day, so I packed a few things and off I went. While on the car ride, I came clean about stealing the pills from my grandmother. That's all I really came clean about because my mother asked me. It made sense. There was suspicion, as I was questioned in the past and denied my involvement.

I was a bit nervous walking into the facility. I never really thought my life would come to this. However, I also walked in with an open mind. I realized that I had a problem. I realized I was an addict. I admitted I was an addict. I just went with the flow and tried to keep everything positive. I didn't want to go in there with a bad attitude because I knew I wouldn't get anything out of it. I really just wanted to get well. That was my main focus. I never wanted to go back to that lifestyle I was living. I didn't want to continue life as a drug addict.

I listened, I followed the rules, and I did what was expected of me. I looked at the whole experience as a once in a lifetime opportunity. I wanted to keep my ears and my mind open. I really wanted to learn more about the disease of addiction and I did. The biggest part of having a fighting chance when leaving detox was being open and honest and taking advice from the counselors. All of the counselors at the McGee Unit were great. I learned a lot from them. They set me on the right path. However, when it was time to leave, all of the decisions were rested upon my shoulders. That was the scary part. I needed a secure aftercare plan and the proper support when leaving the McGee Unit as well.

When talking to the counselors and other patients at the McGee Unit, I identified as an addict. However, I never identified as an alcoholic. I didn't think I had a drinking problem. The only problem that I had involved opiates. That's what I told myself, anyways. I never wanted to use opiates again, but I couldn't picture myself never drinking again. I was only 22 years old. I just couldn't fathom the idea of attempting to wipe the slate clean with booze too. I had my work cut out for me staying clean from opiates alone.

I wasn't really sure of any special type of aftercare plan. I knew I didn't want to go into sober living. That wasn't going to be an option, as I truly believed that I could handle my addiction on my own. Most people, especially professionals in the areas of addiction and alcoholism, might say otherwise. People at the McGee Unit were actually on my side. Patients there thought that I was a young, intelligent man who caught a bad hand. This being my first time in a detox facility, I took everything seriously, and asked questions when needed. Even my counselor had supported my plan to return home. Of course, I would have a plan of my own that would work me towards staying clean and all.

While I was at the McGee Unit, I was given medication to help with the withdrawals I was having. During my stay I only had one 2 mg Suboxone, the medication they use for opiate addiction. This medication blocks the opiate receptors in the brain. It basically made me feel normal. I wasn't craving any opiates when I took that 2 mg tablet. The next four days I just didn't really feel the need for the medication. Of course I wanted it, but I also wanted to have a quick and safe medical detox. The quicker I was off all of the medication, the sooner I would be able to go home. I didn't mind being at the McGee Unit. I'd just rather be home. I wanted to fight this battle on my own terms and I knew it wasn't going to be easy. But I had high hopes. I really did.

I stayed at the McGee Unit for five days, and was released on New Year's Eve. The nurses asked if I wanted to stay another night, as it really wasn't the smartest time to leave. Like they say, there always seems to be a greater temptation to use around the holidays, especially the New Year. However, I felt confident that I would be just fine. I remember waking up in the morning and all of my new found friends, looking to fight their own battles, said their final goodbyes and wished me luck. I still remember all of their faces. It's people like that, people fighting the same fight you're fighting, that you truly never forget. I'm thankful all those faces are still in the back of my head. They truly helped me and I will forever be grateful.

It was snowing like crazy when my father picked me up from the McGee Unit. One of the first things he says involves a certain bottle of booze in the house. Do I really need this shit right now? He asks if I knew anything about a bottle of liquor that was in the closet of the spare bedroom. Of course I did. I drank the entire bottle and threw the bottle away. That's why it was gone. Did I tell him that? Of course not. I just said, "I don't know." My parents really didn't want me to drink when I got home from detox, and I could see that. I don't blame them. I think that's why my father came right out with that question. I just had to make sure I would at least try not to drink. Not right at first. I just got home from detox fighting an opiate addiction, I don't think drinking would be the smartest idea in the book. I even knew that. I took a nap once I walked into my house. That's the first thing I did. I didn't sleep well at the detox facility.

I probably slept a total of ten hours in five nights. It was awful.

Since it was New Year's Eve, my parents had plans to go to my aunt's house. I had no intention of seeing any family, just returning from detox and all. Not to mention I didn't want to show my face to anyone. I still felt a sense of humiliation. I needed a few days to myself. Well, I didn't mind being around my parents, but that's about it. When I pleaded my case to my parents that I would fine by myself, they agreed to give me some space and call me after. I was happy that they trusted me. I'm sitting at my house on my computer when a friend of mine instant messages me. He asks if I want to buy an Oxycontin. It takes me a moment, but I say no. I tell him that I was clean and it was done. Just like that. I guess it really does work. Just say no. I was proud of myself. I actually remember my New Year's Eve of 2008 quite well. I watched all the events they had going on MTV, drank some Gatorade, and took a nice hot bath. That's actually not a bad night. Being home by myself the day of being released from detox, I was able to pass up an offer for Oxycontin and deny any alcoholic beverage. I was proud. I really was, and none of my friends really knew. Well, Pranam knew. My mother informed him of my situation. But nobody really knew where I had been and how I got to where I was. That's the crazy part. I attempted to make my addiction untraceable. In a sense, I did. For most, anyways. But now I couldn't really leave it in the shadows. The fact of the matter is that I'm an addict. I always will be. That's never going to change. People have to know that. I want them to know.

I made it through New Year's Eve without using any drugs or alcohol. It had been a long time since I had carried a single day of sobriety. I never thought about being clean and sober, I didn't really know what that meant. I would spend the next month or so lingering around my house trying to stay away from drugs and alcohol. My main concern was staying away from opiates; alcohol always seemed to stay in the back of my head.

Waking up clean and sober was something I hadn't felt in a

while. I was actually hungry and eager to eat when I woke up. I was no longer reaching for the pills or vomiting in the bathroom. It was such new territory for me that I started to devise a routine for my days. I couldn't just sit at home by myself. I had to get out of the house, at least for a little while each day. I also needed an alternative counterpart to help me out. I began to use chewing tobacco, which seemed to do the trick. Every day I would pack a lip and go for a ride in my car. I would drive the same route, and basically listen to the same songs. I needed that constant daily repetition. It worked well for me. I was staying on track.

About a month into my newfound recovery movement, I began to think about alcohol. I actually began to think about alcohol a lot. I figured my main problem routed from opiates. I was addicted to opiates. That was my only problem. Opiates. Alcohol wasn't a problem for me. When I drank, it wasn't as if I drank every day. I felt that I had a grip on alcohol. Although my prior record would suggest otherwise, I came to the point of saying that I would be fine. I was 22 years old, on the verge of 23. Alcohol couldn't be a problem. Not for me. Not now.

During an afternoon one day, I had this voice in my head that wouldn't stop. It kept telling me to go and buy some alcohol. It kept persuading me to drink. It kept telling me that one drink wouldn't hurt. It kept telling me that everything would be all right. I was contemplating this voice for quite some time until it just took control of me. It wouldn't stop, so I just listened. I began to believe that the voice was true. I got into my car and went to the liquor store. I ended up buying a pint of Southern Comfort and when I got home I drank about half of it within an hour. It knocked me right on my ass and I was in my bed passed out. I woke up in a daze, feeling groggy, but wasn't sick at all. I quite possibly drank the rest of the pint. I'm sure I did. That first official pint would set the trail towards an unhealthy road of drinking. That voice was full of shit!

During my return home from the McGee Unit I had

contacted a doctor to see if I was eligible to be put on the Suboxone program. I really wanted Suboxone as I still felt uncomfortable being without opiates for a short period of time. I felt that they would help me get through the days a bit easier. I figured they would help me with any risks involving relapse. When I was able to get ahold of the doctor's office, which was about an hour drive from my hometown in Shelburne Falls, I was placed on a waiting list. The doctor was only allowed to have a certain number of patients at a given time, hence the waiting list. However, it only took about a month to be accepted. Arriving to my first appointment, I left the office with a prescription for Suboxone.

After taking my first dose of Suboxone, I felt so much better. It kind of made me feel high, in a sense. I didn't let that faze the path I was on. I made sure to take the recommended dose at all times. I never abused the medication. I made sure of that. I did learn a thing or two at the McGee Unit. I wasn't stupid. I didn't want to ever go back to opiates. Ever. It was getting easier to follow the right path and stay clean, but alcohol was beginning to show its ugly face. I began drinking, more and more. And more often.

I soon found myself having a water bottle full of vodka for the drive home from my doctor's visit in Shelburne Falls. It's really when I began this whole phase of pouring straight liquor into clear water bottles. It brings that whole disguise of masking up the appearance of actual water with clear liquor. Everybody would think I was drinking water, that's the whole idea. What if they smelled my breath? There are ways to work around that, but it's basically impossible. I just worried about the whole identity aspect. I was still at the point where I hadn't identified as an alcoholic. So why not hide it? I'm 23 years old and it's only months after coming home clean from opiates when I begin to spiral downhill. Here I am, already drinking straight liquor out of water bottles.

Soon enough, I am drinking every day, and it's not like I'm

just drinking beer. I'm drinking straight liquor, typically the cheap vodka at this point. I am without a job, so I figure straight liquor is the best way to get my money's worth. I could buy a liter of vodka for around $11.00, so that was a bargain in my eyes. I always thought that it would be easy finding a job when I officially graduated from college. That wasn't the case at all. The economy was struggling and so was I. Especially with alcohol.

It is said that you shouldn't drink alcohol while taking Suboxone, but I really didn't care. It didn't seem to have that much of an effect on me. I could still drink as much as I wanted and the medication didn't get in the way. At least that's what I thought. Was it a good idea? Probably not. But I did it. I needed to be able to drink. I just couldn't smoke marijuana because I was drug tested every month while I was taking Suboxone. That's one of the guidelines of being prescribed the medication. I could get away with alcohol, I just had to avoid any and all drugs. That wasn't a problem for me. I was doing a great job staying away from drugs. I was proud of myself for that. It wasn't easy. Alcohol was creeping its way in and I felt that it was beginning to have a grip on me. I guess you could say it already did. I was drinking every day.

My mother was always on my case about finding a job and I really began to become irritated with the constant reminder. It was the spring of 2009 and all I wanted to do was drink. I was struggling financially, as my unemployment check was under $200.00 a week, which left me with only about $60.00 to spend leisurely. Leisurely my ass. That wasn't going to happen, it was all going to be spent on booze. When you only have $60.00, it goes quickly when your only intention is to drink and party.

This whole getting out and looking for a job thing was the last thing that I wanted to do. I had no motivation to go out into the world and look for a job that most likely had nothing to do with the degree I just earned from MCLA. There just weren't many jobs out there. Our economy was in turmoil. Berkshire County was struggling and I didn't want to flip burgers at

McDonald's. I had already done that when I was 14. I wanted a good paying job that was in my field of study. I didn't bust my ass in school for nothing. Whether I was on drugs or not, I still worked hard.

One afternoon my mother comes home from work and is on my ass again to get out and find a job. She brings home some information about a job fair that is taking place in Berkshire County, and I agree to go. I just wanted to stay away from the hassle of constant argument. So the day of the job fair arrives and I get into my car to be on my way. I've already been drinking so I decide to stop at the liquor store and purchase about ten nips of 99 proof schnapps. That was my drink of choice. I loved the flavors, especially blackberries or grape. I either drank 99 proof schnapps or 100 proof peppermint schnapps. Go big or go home, right? It wasn't like I was trying to be a superhero drinker. My tolerance was just so high that I needed the strongest liquor to feel the effect. I could drink a lot. I'll just leave it at that.

While I'm on my way to the job fair, I begin to drink a couple nips and that voice pops in my head again. You know that voice that tells you to just "fuck it, fuck everything." So here I am, contemplating whether or not I'm going to even go to the job fair. I finally arrive to the desired destination and I'm sitting in my car in the parking lot. "This is stupid, I'm not fucking going in there," I tell myself. I come up with the idea that I'll just tell my mother that I went and handed off my resume to a bunch of different companies and that will be that.

I left the parking lot and continued to drink my nips. I killed some time driving around and going into a few stores. I couldn't just go right home. I didn't want to leave any suspicion of not even attempting to go to the job fair. I popped open nip after nip and it began to get dark outside. I was driving drunk and was on my way back home. I mean I was really drunk. I must have drank about eight nips of 99 proof schnapps within two hours. Maybe more, I couldn't tell you. I made it home safely and went to bed. When I woke up in the morning, I was out of alcohol so I got into my car and drove to the liquor store to buy some more booze. While I was inside the liquor store, a fellow citizen that I knew asked me what happened to my car. I had no idea what he was talking about. I went outside to examine my vehicle and noticed there was a small crack in my windshield. I thought that it could be worse. I then looked on the passenger side of the vehicle and saw that the side mirror was missing and the passenger door was completely cracked up. The fender was damaged as well. It wasn't a pleasant sight. How the fuck did this happen? I began to retrace the previous night as vividly as possible. On my way home, although I was completely trashed, I remembered driving over a small bridge and hitting the guardrail. At the time, I thought it would just be a small nick in the car. I was drunk. I had no fucking idea.

I was just happy I dodged a bullet and my parents hadn't noticed the damage to my car as they both left for work in the morning. I had to think quickly and come up with a plan. A different story that would be somewhat believable. I got into my car and called up my brother who was at the house. I told him that I was running an errand and on my way home a deer ran across the road. I told him that I hit the deer and there was damage to my car. My father was about to come home for his lunch break and I made sure to get home before he did. I would explain the whole story to him when he arrived at the house. He was pissed off. I didn't blame him, I was too. The fact of the matter was I hid the fact that I was drinking the night before and it was an alcohol related accident. I didn't want anybody to know what happened. I didn't want anybody, especially my parents, to find out about my alcoholism. I was in denial. I was just happy I didn't get a DUI. It could have been so much worse and I was grateful that it wasn't. I could have killed myself or somebody else. I was totally fucked up that night. I had to keep this a secret. A secret it was. A demon of a secret.

I began working for my best friend Pranam during the

summer of 2009. It was a basic communications job. All I had to do was search for timber in New York counties and areas around New England. I would then contact the owners of that timber and offer them a free timber appraisal. It was basic communication skills, but I struggled, even over the phone. When I worked alone in the office, I would bring nips in my laptop case, drink and make phone calls. Not the best idea, but I did all right. With a little slurred speech, I was transforming into a functioning alcoholic. Everything that I did involved drinking. Hell, I would drink while mowing my grandparents' lawn. Slugging nips while riding the lawnmower. Getting paid $30.00 for cutting the grass only to buy more booze. That's a true alcoholic.

I made decent money working for Pranam but it only lasted a few months. I used one of my paychecks towards a summer vacation in Wildwood, NJ with some friends. One of my friends picked me up at 3 A.M. and I already had my nips in hand. I began drinking the nips once I got in his car. Hey, it was the start of vacation, wasn't it? I thought it was. Drinking every day, all day on vacation was all right. I felt all right because my friends did it too. They were always ready to have a good time. In Wildwood, anything went. No judgment needed. Nobody knew I was an alcoholic who was still taking Suboxone. Maybe they had an idea. At least I didn't smoke weed. I played it safe with my monthly drug tests. We ended up getting kicked out of our hotel on our last night. My friend won a life-sized stuffed animal gorilla. I mean it was just massive. We were all drunk and we ripped out all of the Styrofoam from the inside and made the gorilla into a costume. Soon, most of us were dancing around the hotel in a gorilla suit, our floor covered with chunks of Styrofoam. We then heard a knock at the door and were asked to leave right away. We packed up our stuff and we were gone. At least this didn't happen on our first night. That would've really sucked.

Pranam was running out of work for me to do and soon I

was no longer needed. He also had come to the idea that I was drinking every day. I denied it, but I knew he was right. So here I was again, jobless. I continued drinking on this work-related delay. The good news is that I eventually landed a job in November, 2009 at Dick's Sporting Goods. So, it wasn't that long of a delay. But being without a job, I tended to drink more. So I thought this job would straighten me out a little bit. I was hired as a temporary associate since I would be filling in for a woman on maternity leave. That didn't bother me too much, as there was some speculation that she may not return to the job after all. The position was in my field of work as well, which was a positive aspect in my eyes. I would be working as the Nike Brand Coordinator, which sounded like a cool job in itself. Right up my alley, actually. I loved Nike, and I had a passion for their brand as well. Not quite as passionate as the Jordan brand, but right up there. I was excited to start the job. The company gave me three free Nike polo shirts, along with a brand new pair of Nike sneakers. I had to wear Nike at work, as I represented the brand, and it was cool that the company hooked me up like that. It felt like I was going to be an important employee to the company because I was treated like it. It seemed like things were falling into place for me.

The job itself was your typical sales job in the retail business. I created displays and followed the layout plans for the Nike section of the store. I organized the inventory that was delivered and helped with customer service. It wasn't like I was a manger or anything, so there wasn't a huge weight of responsibility on me. I just had to show up on time and do the work required. It became a bit tedious, doing the same thing day in and day out. So tedious that I soon began drinking booze in my car during my lunch break.

I never got in trouble for drinking or anything of that sort. I was sneaky and got away with it with little suspicion. It wasn't as if I was taking shot after shot after shot in my car. I sipped out of my water bottle and got a buzz. I got along with all of my coworkers, it wasn't a bad job and it turned out that I might be able to stay as a full time employee. Talk about my position went on for a while, so I didn't know if I was going to be able to stay or not.

My hopes were raised and then, just like that, I was told that I had a week left with the company. It wasn't like I was devastated, but it gave me the opportunity to "Just Do It," as Nike would say. Well, my slogan was more like, "Just Fuck It," but that was my whole mentality. During that last week of work, I actually drank inside the workplace. I had nips of 99 proof schnapps in my pockets and I would go into the stockroom and just slug them down. One time I even puked in the stockroom. Luckily nobody saw me. I didn't need any more humiliation in my life. I kept the secret as best as I could. It was like covering up my pill addiction. I didn't want anybody to know about my problem except myself. I was an alcoholic and I was jobless once again.

I lost my job at Dick's Sporting Goods towards the spring of 2010. I was back collecting unemployment checks and my daily drinking was in an uproar. I didn't occupy my time with searching for a job. I put no effort into it. The only effort I put in was if I sent my resume to some companies over the internet. I just felt like I wasn't amounting to anything, after receiving my business degree and all. I thought that my degree would help me and it hadn't. I told myself that it wasn't my fault. It was the economy. So I blamed everything on the economy and drank over the fact that I couldn't even maintain a job.

My drinking was beginning to become problematic and my parents were even growing suspicious. I would be drinking in my room with the door closed and my dad used to walk in and just tell me that it smelled like straight booze. I denied that. Another time, my mother walked into my room when I was taking a sip out of my water bottle and went to hide it under my pillow. She asked me what I was drinking and what I had to hide. I said nothing, trying to get away with it. But she wasn't buying it and demanded to smell its contents, which were straight liquor. I just said whatever, made up some lame excuse. "There's not even a lot in there, I don't drink all the time." I was lying right to her face. I knew I had a problem and she was worried. Deeply saddened that I continued to deny my drinking habits.

I was at a friend's house one day, drinking my usual liquor when I received a phone call from my dad. He basically screamed at me, saying that my mother found a bunch of empty liquor bottles in my bedroom. They had found liquor bottles in the past, and I just used the same excuse as I always had. "I drank those bottle a long time ago, they have been there for months!" I wanted to somehow cover up that my drinking was in the past, that every time they found empty bottles, it wasn't from recent drinking. Somehow I thought that it worked. It was my only excuse! The fact of the matter was that it was getting old. My parents were fed up with all my bullshit, but I didn't care. My parents said that they went through one of my dressers and found like four or five 1 liter bottles of 100 proof peppermint schnapps without a drop of liquor left in them. I'm on the phone telling my father my lame excuse once again and I hang up the phone as his worried voice says goodbye. I smoke some weed out of the hookah and try to forget that confrontation ever happened. But it did. It wasn't the last time I was going to be hearing about it, either.

I remember one time during the summer of 2010, I became really sick. I was throwing up all the time and found it hard to keep food and liquids down. I made an appointment with a Gastroenterologist to get my stomach checked out. Of course I wanted to hide the fact that I was drinking like a fish every day. I got the tests done and I was on my way. I thought everything was all right, as I was beginning to feel a little better. One evening while I'm at the liquor I get a call from my parents saying that the doctor had called back. The doctor stated that I was drinking way too much. My stomach looked awful. If I kept drinking at the pace I was going, I wasn't going to live much longer. I thought it was all a joke. I bought some liquor, went home, closed the door to my room, and drank.

It didn't hit me until one day when my mother walked into my bedroom. "Do you want to kill yourself? You're killing your body, Trev," she said. She talked a little more about this being a lifetime transformation, but I really didn't want to hear that side of the story. I was still, in fact, an active alcoholic. However, something came over me and I didn't want to hurt my parents any more. I didn't really give a shit about myself, but seeing them worried all the time just took a toll on me. I didn't want it to go on any longer. For the first time in my life, I promised my mother that I wouldn't drink. Something inside of me just opened up and my attitude towards keeping this promise was self-assuring. I knew I was capable of keeping a promise, especially to my mother. I knew I could. The hard part would be staying away from that next drink. I don't know why, but I gave it a shot. I wanted to at least try. It was August, 2010.

That moment I promised that I wouldn't drink, I left the house to give my brother a ride to work. I smoked a little pot with him and called my father to see if it would be all right if I could hang at my friend's for a while. He didn't mind, but soon enough my mother called me once I arrived at my friend's. She said that I needed to be home. I needed to be in a safe environment, away from any temptation of alcohol. I promised that I wasn't going to drink. That was my plan. But who knows what would've happened. I listened to my mother and went home. I didn't drink that night. A week went by and I was completely sober. Not a drop of alcohol touched my mouth. The only thing I did was smoke marijuana. I felt like I needed something to replace the alcohol with. So I smoked pot from time to time. I didn't think it was that big of a deal. Just some pot here and there. At least I wasn't drinking or doing any crazy drugs.

On September 5, 2010 my mother sent me message over the computer. It read:

Trev, I am so very proud of you. We all love you so much! Keep up the good work and your life will be so much better. You're one great son, and we are all on your side! Love you!!!

I was beginning to repair that whole relationship with not only my mother, but my entire family. I was given much needed support, which helped me stay sober. I made a conscious effort to stay away from the whole bar scene and from parties in general. Soon enough, I tested my limits and began to go to parties, but I stayed sober. I just smoked pot. I was doing good. I was even counting my days of being sober. It was a good feeling, adding up day after day. It was an accomplishment and I was proud of myself. Some of my friends couldn't believe I was actually staying sober. Some figured out that it was probably my parents that made me get sober, and in most ways it was. I was just doing the work. I was the one making the decisions. I started to gain some self-control and it was a good feeling. My parents were no longer worrying about me. They were happy for me. Always rooting for me. They were always in my corner.

There was always some temptation, of course, when I was around alcohol. I didn't really have a plan on how long I would actually stay sober for. I just took it day by day. I couldn't picture myself without ever being able to drink again, and that's what really got to me. I didn't have a proper foundation set up for my sobriety. First of all, I was smoking pot every day, which is never a good thing to do when trying to get sober. I'm not saying it's a bad thing. People do it. I know people who are still sober today, but still use marijuana. I just always felt that it wouldn't last forever. For me, anyways. And I was right.

I was 58 days sober when I met up with some friends to go to a Kid Cudi concert in Springfield, MA on October 23, 2010. Kid Cudi was and still is my favorite musical artist of today's era, and I was beyond excited to be going to see him perform live. I drove up with a few friends from my hometown and we met some other friends at Western New England College (WNEC).

We stopped at the liquor store and before entering I had this urgent feeling that overcame my whole body. It was like my bloodstream was screaming "Alcohol!" That voice popped in my head again. It said, "Trevor, you're going to drink today." It wouldn't stop. I even told my friends that I might end up drinking. Of course they didn't want me to, but at the same time, they weren't totally against the idea. They weren't going to stop me if I chose to drink. Even if they tried, I wouldn't let them. I had that mentality in my head and it was overwhelming. Overpowering.

When we got back to our friend's dormitory, everyone began drinking in celebration for the anticipated performance later on in the evening. I thought to myself that I would just play a few drinking games with my friends. A few drinks never hurt anyone, I thought. That first Twisted Tea tasted so good. I had a few drinks within an hour and I had a good buzz going. I felt great, so I continued to drink before the concert.

On the way to the concert, I smoked some marijuana, and decided that I would hide my bowl piece in my shoe and sneak some pot in. It worked. The concert was amazing, and we were all enjoying ourselves. I smoked a few bowls and halfway through the concert I began to feel a bit dizzy. The area where we were standing was crowded, so I decided to head towards the back of the venue and get some space. The whole room was just spinning and before I knew it, I fainted. I cracked my face off a wooden table, and instantly regained consciousness. I was still in a haze, and did my best to stand up straight. People were staring at me, as blood was pouring off my face. Nobody attempted to help me or ask if I was all right. I just stood there, hoping that the bleeding would stop. The bleeding eventually stopped as I held my nose with my hands and the concert ended. My friends walked to the back of the venue and there I was, standing like I just got my ass kicked by some stranger. However, that wasn't the case. I think it was the fact that I drank a lot and smoked after 58 days of sobriety. The alcohol just hit me like a freight train, and my face could hold some evidence to that.

When I arrived back to my friend's dorm, we had some laughs, ordered some food and went to bed. The next morning, I wake up and there's a bottle of Jagermeister sitting in the room. I take a few sips and we go to the sports bar to watch some football. I drink a few beers and on the ride back to our hometown I drink a few more Twisted Teas. I'm back at square one and I knew it. I fucked up. I was back to drinking every day. I didn't want to tell my parents what had happened, so I kept it to myself. I was extra careful if I was drinking in my room and made sure no empty liquor bottles were lingering around to be found. I soon began going out on weekends, as my parents probably thought I was doing good, but I was drinking. I tried to be a little smarter with the whole aspect of my drinking routine, but I was an alcoholic. I couldn't hide it forever. I found a way to show my parents that I could handle alcohol. I was soon drinking a few beers, here and there, around my family. I made it look easy. The fact of the matter is that I was a functioning alcoholic. I could drink as much liquor as I wanted by myself, and still be able to have a few beers with the family. They didn't know that I fell back into that slump of drinking straight liquor. They thought I was just drinking a few beers. That's how I portrayed myself. A beer drinker. I was damn good at it.

As I began drinking heavily alone, I made sure to keep all of my empty liquor bottles in my vehicle and lock the doors. That way nobody could get inside besides me. I would then drive to a desolate area and dump the bottles. It was simple as that. I may have been killing the ozone, but it was worth not getting caught by my parents. I would drink and drive all the time. It was a normal thing to me. I became really good at it, if that actually makes sense. It's nothing to brag about. Everywhere I went, I had a water bottle full of booze in my vehicle. It was sad.

About a month after my relapse, I applied for a job at Hillcrest Educational Centers. I was hired that month as a Youth Development Counselor and I was a bit anxious to start this job. I would be working with children and young adults from the ages of 10 to 21. These kids have all had tough pasts. Most were traumatized and had been victims of physical and/or sexual abuse. My job was basically to maintain a professional and supportive relationship. I also had to provide them with coping tools to help them not only get through the day, but to succeed. A difficult job? Yes, and there was a lot of training involved, including CPR, first aid, and TCI restraint training, which would allow me to safely restrain the youth when necessary. A lot of patience was required in this line of work. I was lucky I had it.

I would work Wednesday, Thursday, and Friday from 2:45 to 11 P.M. On Saturday, my shift started at 8 A.M and went until 11 P.M. I worked the residential shift, so I basically was in their care from when the kids got out of school until they went to bed. It was a pretty hectic shift, but I got Sunday, Monday, and Tuesday off every week. The pay wasn't the greatest and the commute wasn't much better. I had to travel from Adams to Great Barrington, which is close to an hour ride. In the end, that all didn't matter to me. Working for Hillcrest was one of the best things I ever did with my life. It was a life changer. I learned a great deal, probably more than I ever did in college. However, there was still a problem. I was an alcoholic working with some of the toughest kids to handle. Nobody knew that but me.

I would drink straight nips of booze before my shift every day. I would wake up at like 9:30 A.M. and drink like five or six nips, spread out between then and the time I had to leave my house at 1:30 P.M. I would often drink out of my water bottle full of straight liquor on the way to work as well. It was an hour drive, after all. Halfway through my ride I would stop drinking and load up with mints and gum, attempting to dissolve the scent of any alcohol. I would get to work and make sure I didn't breathe around anyone and kept my talking limited. When I got to the floor and began working with the kids, I acted like my normal self. I took my job seriously. I loved the kids. I really did. I cared about them. I was just a functioning alcoholic that provided this love and this care.

I got along with all of my coworkers. It was like we were this tight knit family working for Hillcrest. We all worked together, as a team, which was real nice. I don't want to get too in-depth about the whole organization, I just want to talk about my experience with the company. Of course I had a drinking problem, which I tried to hide. There were times when I went on break and drove off campus to the liquor store to purchase a few nips of peppermint schnapps. I would drink them before I returned to work and act as if nothing happened. Crazy, stupid shit like that happened. It was my choice, but it was the disease controlling me.

I was asked multiple times to talk with the Residential Coordinator about rumors of my drinking. He would have me come to his office and he would tell me that someone had smelled alcohol on my breath. I would deny it every time, and I was off the hook. Just like that. But how long could this last? I loved these kids, and I didn't want to lose my job over my alcoholism. I was just on a continual downward spiral. The kids had no idea what I was pulling, not even the employees did. Nobody deserved to have someone like me working for them. Especially these kids. I don't care how much they liked me. I continued to drink before work every day. I would come home from work and drink myself to bed.

I spent a lot of money on alcohol. I would usually stock up twice a week, but I was in the liquor store nearly every day of the week. When I stocked up I would get two liters of 100 proof peppermint schnapps, one 750 ml of 99 proof schnapps, and six to eight nips of 99 proof schnapps. It would last me a couple of days and then I would end up back at the liquor store. I ran my own tab at the liquor store so when I received my pay check from Hillcrest every two weeks, which was approximately $740.00, I would pay off my tab, which was usually around $200.00. I would then give $500.00 to my mother and I would keep what was left. Hence, I needed the tab. I had created my own system to supply my habit and keep my mother off my back with money issues.

It didn't take too long for my parents to become suspicious again. The smell of booze in my room and hidden water bottles full of liquor were just a few signs of my problem. Of course, I denied the fact that I had a problem, but I agreed to talk to a psychologist once a week. The first time I met with Dr. Siracusa, my parents joined me. Concerns were laid out on the table, but I still had the desire to drink. I listened to what was said. How my parents wanted to see me happy and healthy again. The whole nine yards about how this disease was killing me. I was getting the hint that I did, in fact, have a problem with alcohol. Dr. Siracusa was a very nice man: genuine, honest, and nonjudgmental. He set up a weekly group meeting where I would meet with other people struggling with alcohol. I said that I would give it a chance.

On May 3, 2011 my mother sent me a message over the computer. It read:

Hi, I think our first session went very well yesterday. I am proud of the man you are, and I truly believe you can beat your bad drinking habits. We all love you and will stand by your side always. Love you.

It was nice to see that my family was in my corner rooting for me, but I wasn't fighting. When I showed up to my first group meeting, there were other people there that had been working hard on their drinking problems. It kind of intimidated me. How are these people actually doing this? Dr. Siracusa asked me what I wanted to get out of this group. I said that I wanted to cut down on my drinking. It was known that I drank every day, so the first step was to focus on not drinking one out of the seven days of the week. When I would come back to the next group, I would say that I didn't drink Saturday. In a sense, it was kind of true. I would work from 8 A.M. until 11 P.M. and wouldn't get home until midnight. So in a sense that was true. If I wasn't drinking on the ride home. And that never happened. So I guess you could say, I *almost* didn't drink for a full day. One of the guys in the group asked me if I was addicted to alcohol. I think I said probably. When I left the group meeting, I got into my vehicle and drank out of my water bottle full of booze. I guess you could say I was.

I ended up skipping a few meetings, and something came in the mail that said I owed $100.00 for missing my appointment. My mother found it and was pissed. I called the office and I told them I forgot to cancel because I was really sick. I just made it up to clear the $100.00 bill. That was besides the fact. I was an alcoholic refusing any form of help.

On April 20, 2011 my mother became very concerned. She wrote me a very emotional and powerful letter over the computer. It read:

Hi, Trev. I don't know what to do anymore, I just feel that I have failed you as a mom. You're sick and you need help, and I should have been on you every second from 5 years ago or longer. I am sick, so sick that you're killing yourself, and you're going to die on me and I would just not want to live anymore if that happened. I know you can't help it, it's an addiction, a bad disease, something that won't go away without professional help. I want you to tell me what I can do for you. You're my baby who I love so much. I am not angry, I am sad, so sad that you're going through this, needing a drink, a bottle, every day. I have tried to talk to you face to face and you just lie to me. I am hoping that this will make it easier for you to communicate with me. Let me know what I can do, and don't say you're fine, you're not. Don't say you don't drink much or won't drink. You will. Don't say you will go to AA, you said that four months ago. I want you to tell me "you went" to AA, that you need help, and it will be a struggle and a long road. I will be at your side, your dad will be at your side, your family loves you, they want you to be healthy and happy. Please understand how hard it is for me to see you killing yourself daily. I am sorry, I hope you can forgive me for not dragging you somewhere when I should have. You're an adult, I can't "make you" do something, but I can certainly make you stop killing yourself. I will force you if I have to, but I don't want to. So please, I am begging you to get help, step one: go to AA, soon, real soon. If you want me to go or your dad or both, we will, but please go. You don't have to talk to me, you just need to first admit you're an alcoholic and from there you will start your road to recovery. Love you with all my heart.

I continued to drink everyday after reading that letter. It was Sunday, May 13, 2012. Mother's Day. I was at my grandmother's house celebrating Mother's Day with the family, having a few drinks. For some reason, I got the urge to try to get a hold of some Suboxone. I don't know why, since I had been off the medication for quite some time now. Anyways, I contacted a friend and he said that he would be able to hook me up later on that day. Some other friends called me up and asked if I wanted to play some drinking games with them. I made sure I spent some time with my family, especially my mother, and had some lunch with everyone. I then told my family that I was going to meet up with some friends for the day. It was all good. When I got to my friend's house, I began drinking some Twisted Teas and some 99 blackberries (99 proof schnapps, my signature drink). I also smoked some weed and it was such a beautiful day outside. Blue skies and sunshine. I began discussing what kind of vehicle I was going to purchase in the near future with my friends. I had finally saved up a decent amount of money and was looking for a new vehicle. A few hours later, my other friend contacts me about the Suboxone and says that he had one for me. I left my friends and went en route towards the Suboxone.

When I got to my friend's, I asked if he could spot me the Suboxone and I would pay him back. He had no problem with that and I snorted half of the pill. I returned to my other friend's house and continued to drink. I kept drinking my 99 blackberries, maybe even 99 grapes and chased them down with 24 oz. Twisted Teas. We were all playing cards, having a good time. Then one of my friends decided to leave, and rather than staying to at least sober up, I decided to leave as well. I knew that I had liquor stashed away somewhere in my bedroom. I got into my Chevy Blazer with no hesitation and drove down the steep driveway. I was completely fucked up. I knew it and I could feel it. Mixing all that alcohol and snorting that Suboxone really fucked me up. I had no intention of stopping my vehicle or pulling over. I began to gain some speed as I approached a stop sign. I could take a left or a right and figured I would take a right. It would be less risky. Away from any potential cops. However, as I approached the stop sign I didn't slow down all that much. I jerked hard to the right and my steering wheel locked up.

The side of my vehicle crashed into the telephone pole across the street and I began to panic. No vehicles were in the streets and there was no sight of any that were oncoming. I paused for a second and thought, "Oh fuck, I have to get out of this situation!" I backed up and hit a mailbox. I continued to back up across the entire street and hit the guardrail for about 15 feet until I finally stopped. Not knowing what to do, I get off the road and go back in the direction of my friend's house. As I turn around, not knowing all of my tires are popped, my face hits the side of the passenger door, I come up out of my seat, and end up in the front passenger's seat, covered in glass.

I really didn't know what had happened until I opened my eyes. My vehicle did a complete barrel roll and landed in a grassy area on the side of the road. I was sitting in the passenger's seat and I couldn't move. I knew I didn't break any bones, but still I couldn't move. It was as if all the life was sucked out of me. I tried to get up and move towards the driver's seat a few times, but I didn't have the strength. I just sat there for a little while and waited for any strength that I had to enter back into my body. When I finally managed to move myself from the passenger's seat to the driver's seat, I heard a voice from the outside of the vehicle. "Don't move, there's help on the way," she said. The woman then climbed into the back of my vehicle and held my head straight. She told me not to move my head as I could have injured my neck in the accident. She was an EMT who wasn't on her shift and happened to arrive at the scene.

I told the woman that I was fine, and I attempted to turn the keys in the ignition as if the engine would start. The woman said that my vehicle wasn't going to start any time soon. It was completely totaled. I just sat inside my vehicle and waited for the ambulance to arrive. Although I felt that I could walk away from the accident without a problem, I knew it would be impossible to talk my way out of it. The only apparent injury that I had was an abrasion to my forehead. I was a little bruised up, but no serious injuries occurred. I was lucky. I mean real lucky. I could have broken my neck. I can still picture my head hitting the side of the window and bouncing off the ground. Somebody was looking out for me. I think it could have quite possibly been my friend Tommy Oxton, God rest his soul.

The ambulance arrived and the paramedics strapped me to the stretcher. On the way to the North Adams Regional Hospital, one of the paramedics asked me if I took any drugs. He said that he wouldn't tell the cops, so I told him that I snorted some Suboxone. I was still pretty fucked up from the booze and the Suboxone, but I was coherent.

The ambulance ride felt like I was in a video game, but I wasn't the one holding the controller. I had no control. I only had three questions on my mind. "How the fuck did I end up in this situation?" "Why me?" and, "Am I going to get away with it?" When I finally got to the hospital, the doctor was prepping me for a CAT scan and called his partner over to take a look into my eyes. The doctor states, "Just look at his eyes. It's easy to tell." He was referring to how fucked up I was.

After the CAT scan, a police officer came in with a liter bottle of 100 proof peppermint schnapps that was almost empty and said he found it in my vehicle. I admitted it was mine. It was funny because the whole time, I thought I was getting away with this whole situation I was in. Nobody ever took my driver's license, and I was never given a breathalyzer test. However, my blood was taken at the hospital. I didn't know what for at the time because nobody clarified what I was signing for. Either way, I still had the mentality that everything was going to be all right. I was even talking to a worker at the hospital as I stated, "I'm not really mad that I totaled my vehicle because I was in the process of buying a new one." How crazy is that?

The nurse finally said that I was free to leave, and that's when I really felt that I was off the hook. I called up my friend to pick me up and I stayed at their house. It was the same place where I was just drinking before I got into the accident. I went into the house, sat on the couch, reached inside my pockets and found a nip of 99 proof schnapps. I slugged it down and contemplated what I was going to tell my parents.

I wrote a message to my mother over the computer and this is exactly what it said:

Hey mom I was I'm a car accident tonight and it had to be towed to route 8 they said it may be totaled so I had to go to the er to get checked out...just a few cuts SO they let me go and Libby picked me up so. sleepin there..luckily I.was not drinking...my steering wheel locked up. And hit a telephonwe pole...I'm ok so don't worry o will call u at work tomorrow...love ya

That's what I remember happening to the best of my

ability. The actual incident report (police report) came later.

When I woke up in the morning my friend Jake brought me home. Looking at the gash on my forehead, he says, "Don't you think you should probably try to stop drinking?" Of course I say that I fucked up and maybe I should consider it. However, once I get home, I go right to my bedroom and start drinking 100 proof peppermint schnapps straight out of my water bottle. The same water bottle I was trying to drive home to the previous night. We all know that I didn't make it too far.

My father came home for his lunch break around 11 A.M. and I tell him my bullshit story. He buys it. But for the next week, questions keep arising, and suspicion grows. I still have the frame of mind that I got away with a DUI and am in complete denial about my alcoholism. I don't have to go to work until Wednesday so my father bring me down to clean out my wrecked vehicle. He doesn't know that I actually barrel rolled the vehicle so when he sees the damage, he is completely stunned. "I can't believe you didn't kill yourself," he says. I couldn't either. I'm telling you, Tommy was looking out for me. I truly believe that he was the one who saved my life that night.

After I clean out my vehicle and get all my possessions, my father continues to question me on the ride home. He says, "Are you sure you weren't drinking that night?" I tell him no. How many times did I have to tell him? My story wasn't going to change and the suspicion only grew. In the eyes of my parents, something wasn't adding up.

While I was at work on Wednesday, my mother left me a message to call her and she said it was important. I called her and she said that something came in the mail relating to the accident. It was something about property damage from a citizen, and the suspicion just kept growing. I kept telling my parents that everything was all right. I told them that I wasn't drinking. I went to work Thursday and woke up Friday morning with my mother in disappointment. A citation for my DUI came in the mail that was sitting in plain view on the kitchen table. I had nowhere to go. I was caught. My denial was no longer a useful tool. My heart sank, but the only thing I cared about was alcohol.

My mother had to get out of the house and go for a walk because she was in such disappointment. I took my cousin's vehicle, which I was using at the time, and went to the liquor store. I came back with a 750 ml bottle of 99 proof schnapps and drank as I tried to find a coworker to pick me up for work. My parents weren't going to let me drive. I knew that for a fact. I continued to drink heavily every day, holding on to my job and finding rides to and from the workplace. I was still a functioning alcoholic. I knew how to make things work out. I knew I had to. Or I would lose my job. I needed to keep my job. It was the only good thing going for me in my life. I still loved my job. I loved the kids I worked with. But I had a drinking problem, and nobody really knew the hell I was living in.

There was a day at work a few months later when I was just not my normal self. I was a functioning alcoholic, but I wasn't functioning too well on this particular evening shift. My body was just spent. All the drinking was catching up to me. I was in a sort of daze. I wasn't alert. I just wasn't all there. To make a long story short, we have cameras everywhere at Hillcrest. So my behavior was noticed as I wasn't acting like my normal self, attempting to open closet doors with a pen. I was asked to go down to the supervisor's office towards the end of shift, and I was just sitting there wondering what was going on. I didn't know why I was down there, as my supervisor asked me, "Skrock, is everything all right?" I said that I was fine and just sat there in anticipation.

One of my coworkers got off the phone and asked me to go outside to smoke a cigarette, so I went with him. He told me that he just got off the phone with the Residential Coordinator and said that I may be losing my job. I had no idea why. I had no idea what was going on. So my boss shows up at the end of shift and tells me that he has to bring me to the lab to take a drug and alcohol test. I agreed to do so and admitted I had used marijuana a few days prior. Anyhow, I passed the alcohol test and had to wait for the drug test. Since it was a Wednesday, I wasn't allowed to come back to work until the results came in. I came up with an excuse and told my parents I was staying at a friend's and he was bringing me to work for the next couple days. I was in fact just drinking, smoking, and partying on my days away from work.

I remember just staying away from home on my suspension from work because I didn't want my parents to know what was going on. One day I had a friend bring me to North Adams to meet up with another friend. I had a bottle of liquor in a paper bag and I was just walking around North Adams, waiting for my friend to get home. When he called me and told me I could come over, I ended up walking into the wrong house and began calling his name. Nobody answered and before I knew it a man walks in while I'm standing alone in his kitchen. I was drunk, but somehow I sweet talked my way out of it. I'm just lucky he didn't kick my ass or call the cops.

When I finally made it to the actual house that my friend lived at, I began to drink my bottle of booze. He said that he was going to get some Percocets and something in my blood began to run wild. I told him that I would buy two Percocets, and that's exactly what I did. I wasn't on probation or anything yet, as my court case kept being pushed back. I didn't have to worry about any drug tests, so my brain was going crazy, basically telling me to feed it. I relapsed that day, after nearly four years clean. I snorted both Percocets, drank my booze, and smoked some pot. I totally lost control that day. My back had been against the wall for so long that I just had to let go.

Fortunately, I haven't touched an opiate since that day.

Tuesday rolls around and my boss calls me. He says, "Skrock, you're good. You can come back to work tomorrow. We will pay you for the days that you missed. Sorry for the trouble." I was ecstatic. It was as if I'd gotten away with murder. Now I could drink and not have to worry about losing my job. Crazy as that sounds, it's how I felt. It made life a little easier to tolerate. Now, I just had to face the court system in regards to my DUI conviction. But I would meet with my lawyer first.

When I met with my lawyer, we went over what I could expect from the court case. It was in my best interest to just plead guilty and try to get some stuff wiped off the incident. For instance, I wasn't wearing a seat belt, I admitted I was speeding, and I was up for marked lanes violations as well. Maybe some of these things could go away. Since my parents went with me to meet with my lawyer, they were given a copy of the incident report (police report). My mother began to read it in the car. I was humiliated as I listened to the whole story. After all of the denial. After the suspicion had kept growing. My lies were just lies and the facts were in black and white. I felt ashamed, and I knew I couldn't help it. I had a controlling disease.

Here is the summary of the police report. The officer wrote:

On Sunday, May 13, 2012, I was on patrol and dispatched to report of a single motor vehicle accident rollover vs. tree. I arrived on scene and observed the vehicle, a blue Chevy Blazer, in the grass. I observed the sign and pole for Sandmill Road had been knocked over. There was one member of the Cheshire Fire Department and the homeowners that called 911 to report the accident on scene prior to my arrival. I observed the vehicle on all four tires and it had sustained heavy damage as a result of the multiple collisions the vehicle was involved in. As I approached the vehicle, I was approached by two people. The first was the reporting party.

"I heard brakes squealing and looked out my bedroom window. I saw the car up against the telephone pole and mailbox across the street. The car reversed and hit the mailbox and tree across the other side of the street. Then it proceeded forward, hitting guardrails near Sandmill Road, and rolled over. I walked over to the car and driver. He was in the

passenger seat. I asked him if he was all right and he said yes. I was standing in the driver's side window and there was a strong odor of alcohol."

The other person to approach me was a Cheshire Fire Fighter.

"At around 9:30 P.M. the Cheshire Fire Department was dispatched for a one car motor vehicle accident with reported personal injury and a rollover. I was the first one on scene other than the homeowners that called it in. The party was the sole occupant of the blue Chevy Blazer. The homeowner stated the party was trying to restart the vehicle despite the condition. I told the party who I was and my rank and asked him not to attempt to move the vehicle. The party did not respond and continued to turn the key. I asked if he had been drinking and he said he had been drinking at a friend's house in Cheshire. He said he was unsure how much and laughed. He stated he could not remember, as it was a lot. After going over medical history with the party, he became agitated. He started pushing my hands away from his neck and demanded I give him his keys. I informed him they were not in my possession and the party began to exit the vehicle. It is then that additional emergency personnel assisted in boarding the party."

As the operator was being boarded, I asked him if he was injured and he stated, "My neck hurts." His voice was extremely slurred and he had watery, glassy and bloodshot eyes. I observed him to have numerous abrasions on his face. I asked him if he was wearing his seat belt and he stated "No." Skrocki was then secured in the Adams ambulance and transported to the North Adams Regional Hospital. I advised the barracks to send a flat bed for the vehicle. Per MSP towing policy, I inventoried the vehicle. I immediately smelled a strong odor of an alcoholic beverage upon entering the driver's side door. During the course of the motor vehicle inventory, I discovered an open bottle of Peppermint Schnapps that was 4/5ths empty. The bottle was located in the pocket behind the passenger seat.

I left the accident scene and proceeded to North Adams Regional Hospital to speak with Trevor Skrocki. I entered the emergency room and a nurse advised me he was in room 2. The door was open to room 2 and immediately I detected a strong odor of an alcoholic beverage as I *entered the doorway. I observed Trevor Skrocki laying on the hospital bed and he was on his back. He had a neck brace secured around his neck. I announced and identified myself and he told me to come inside the room. I walked up to him and asked if he had any injuries and he stated, "My neck hurts." I observed his eyes to be extremely watery, glassy and bloodshot. I detected a very strong odor of an alcoholic beverage emanating from his breath and his speech was extremely slurred. I asked Trevor Skrocki if he would consent to a blood test for the presence of alcohol and he stated, "No." I asked him to tell me what happened and he verbally stated, "I was driving too fast on Sandmill Road and crossed the road and hit a pole. I think I backed up and hit a mailbox. The last thing I remember was hitting the guardrail and rolling over." I asked him where he was coming from and he stated "My friend's house on Sandmill Road. But I'm not telling you whose." I asked him how much he had to drink and he stated "I'm sure you found the bottle of schnapps in the vehicle."*

These details of the incident actually occurred and I was in such denial that I didn't want to believe them to be true.

I received a message from my cousin's wife on September 11, 2012. She wrote me a powerful letter. It read:

Trevor, I'm writing to you because I care and I want you to get better. You don't have to respond and you probably won't like what I have to say, but I'm going to say it anyways because I don't want to see you in jail or dead. You have a disease and you need help. You are so smart, you have a wonderful job, and a family who loves you so much. Like you I spent almost a year of my life fighting a disease that was killing me. I went through eight months of hell and every day I prayed that I would live to see my daughter grow up. It breaks my heart and it makes me so angry that you are not willing to put up that fight and beat this disease. You have the help at your fingertips, but only YOU can make the decision to use it. You have so much to offer in this world. You have friends and a family that want you in their lives. I'm praying that

someday very soon you will choose the help.
Love you, Emily.

I met with my lawyer before I was to go in front of the judge. A different judge had been there that day so my lawyer pled the case that I had the right to see the original judge. When I left the courtroom, he asked to talk to me and my parents in his office. He said, "Trevor, when you show up to court next, don't drink." He smelled alcohol on my breath and I left the court room carrying a sense of disgrace. On the ride home, my parents pleaded that I stop drinking. Stop drinking for good. I couldn't.

So I pled guilty and my time in front of the judge had arrived. I made sure I didn't drink the night before so my breath wouldn't smell like booze. I was placed on two years probation. I lost my license for two years. I would have random drug and alcohol screenings. I would have to take outpatient classes for a year. I would also have to attend a 14-day impatient treatment program in Tewksbury, MA.

I began probation in October, 2012 and continued to drink every day and smoke weed on occasion. I passed my first drug test and my time was coming when I would be leaving for Tewksbury, MA. I would be leaving the Sunday after Thanksgiving so I guess you could say that I had some time to prepare. The 14-day program sent me a packet of what I was to expect. I glanced over it, and never really read it thoroughly.

I was working Friday night and I realized that I would be going away Sunday. I had to work a 15 hour shift on Saturday and I didn't really have any time for myself. I got home from work on Friday night and laid down in my bed slugging nips of liquor. Then all of a sudden I said, "Fuck it." I called up work and told them that I wouldn't be in on Saturday because I was sick. I walked out of my house and down to the bars to meet up with some friends. I got drunk and stayed over at a friend's house smoking weed until 6 A.M. I slept at her house for a few hours, woke up and went right to the liquor store.

I drank from morning till night and ended up at a bar for a black light party. It was about 11 P.M. when I was talking to a friend who had previously attended the 14-day program in Tewksbury. She said, "Why are you drinking? You know they give you a breathalyzer test before you are allowed to enter Tewksbury." I was in shock and just went right home, not consuming another sip of alcohol. My arrival time wasn't until 12 P.M. so I had about 12 hours to blow a .00. I was still nervous as hell, and when I woke up at 8 A.M. my parents and I were soon on the road for a three hour drive.

When I arrived at Tewksbury I was waiting in my parents' vehicle and my mom was saying that they were going to give me a breathalyzer test. She asked if I was going to be all right and I said that I didn't know. Another shocker for my concerned parents. I was living in a hell, praying that I would pass this stupid test. Please, God.

I walked into the place and it was soon my turn to take the breathalyzer test. I blew into the device and I soon saw the readings go from .03 to .04. I told the guy that the machine must be messed up and he let me blow into the device again. Again, .03, .04. I was fucked. They asked me to wait over to the side where they wrote down some information for my probation officer. I pleaded like a little baby asking for a chance. Just one chance. Just let me into the program. I didn't need any more shame in my life!

Since my parents left for a little while to grab a bite to eat before they said their final goodbyes, I made a phone call to tell my mother the disappointing news. My parents drove back and waited in the parking lot as I walked out with my luggage looking like a lost soul. I felt worthless. I had never felt so much damn pity for myself. I just sat in the backseat as my parents yelled and yelled and yelled. "You're probably going to end up going to jail, Trev!" "No, I'm not! Don't fucking worry about it," I hollered back. It was a long three hour drive back home. A long, miserable ride.

When I got home, my parents went downstairs to the basement and I went into my mother's bedroom to get some wine. I was all out of booze. My mother previously found my stash of booze in my shoe boxes. I got home one night from work and went to get some liquor and it was gone. She also found all of my empty bottles. I put them all under my dresser. I thought it was a good hiding place, since I had been doing it for months, disposing of the bottles as the area got full. This time it was full to the max and my mother must have found at least ten bottles and sixty nips. All empty.

So I got a few small bottles of wine from my mother's closet and went into my room to drink. I drank about three or four little bottles and needed more. I knew the closet in the living room that contained the liquor was locked, but I knew where the key was. It was on a keychain with about twenty other keys, so I would have to experiment with trial and error. Nonetheless, I waited for the right opportunity when my mother went to bed and my father was resting downstairs. I grabbed the keys and went to work as quietly as I could. When I finally got the door open, I grabbed a bottle of Bacardi and locked it back up. I went into my room, closed the door, and drank.

When I woke up in the morning, I figured that I would just have to call my probation officer and let him know what happened. However, my father had a different idea. He was going to make me go down to the courthouse and confront my probation officer. "Here we go again," I thought. I was just drinking the night before so I made sure to scrounge up as much time as I could to sober up. I took a long shower and when I was ready my father drove me down to the courthouse.

When I got out of the vehicle and started walking towards the courthouse entrance my father says, "What's the matter, Trev?" I didn't know. I had no expression. I had no feelings. I had no emotion inside of me. I was silent and I walked through the doors like a ghost. I walked in as if nobody could even see me. Nobody could see my pain. I was there, but my spirit was gone.

I walked up to my probation officer and showed him the information from Tewksbury. He said that I violated my probation and I would have to see the judge today. I remember my father telling my probation officer, "He's sick, he can't help it." My probation officer then asked me to blow into the breathalyzer. I agreed and prayed that I was sober. He didn't show me what the test read, and he never told me that I failed. So I didn't know if I actually passed or if he was giving me a break. In any case, I didn't really know what was going to happen. When I finally got in front of the judge, my probation officer recommended that I get the harshest punishment. He wanted to throw me in jail. I was just sitting there, hopeless, waiting for the verdict.

The judge was reading through some material but couldn't find the proper writing to throw me in jail. Something inside me said that I may have a chance. I was to go directly to the McGee Unit as soon as possible and I agreed. Something opened my eyes. This was a blessing in disguise. I was sitting there, ready to go to jail and all of a sudden I was given the opportunity to go back to the detox center at the McGee Unit. The place that saved my life from opiates. I couldn't believe it. Through all the bumps in the road, I never thought I would keep getting up after I kept falling down. After this moment of clarity, I stayed up and I moved forward. I was thankful. Somebody up there didn't want to see me die. Somebody wanted to see me have another shot at life. Somebody wanted me to learn from my mistakes, rather than sit in jail cell.

I went home from the courthouse and awaited a call from the McGee Unit. My best friend Pranam came over to see me and say goodbye. Pranam was the only friend who really stayed by my side throughout my addictions. I remember sitting in my room drinking and he would call me up. I wouldn't answer. Then he would just show up at my house and walk through the door.

He wanted to see how I was doing. I hated it at the time, but he was the only friend who gave a shit. He was the one friend who was hopeful. He wanted to see me as the original Trevor Skrocki. He knew I could do it, and he wanted to see me change. I thank him so much. He was always there. That's a true friend.

When the McGee Unit finally called, I said goodbye to Pranam and he wished me luck. My parents drove me to the hospital and I was soon inside the McGee Unit. I was back again, fighting for my life. I went in there with an open mind and a positive attitude. I knew I wouldn't have a chance if I even thought about drinking again. I was there to learn. I was there to listen. I was there to get well. That's it. I wanted a new life. That's what saved me last time. That's how I escaped opiate addiction. I *wanted* to change. I *wanted* to be free. I just wanted to be Trevor Skrocki again.

I remember being at the McGee Unit one night and they had an NA (Narcotics Anonymous) meeting. I was one of two people that showed up to the meeting. Everybody else, maybe twelve other people, were in their beds. The speakers said, "Thank you both for showing up. Without you guys, we wouldn't be able to do this." I was making an effort. I knew I was. I was going to every meeting and all the groups. I didn't miss anything, and I always showed up on time.

I stayed at the McGee Unit for about five days and was discharged on a Saturday. I came out with a positive attitude and I was grateful for the opportunity to better myself. Detox is just one of the first steps of getting well, and I still had to confront the fact that I was an alcoholic. That's exactly what I did when I got home. My father and I went to an AA meeting that night and I also went to another meeting the following morning. I knew I was an alcoholic, that's why I was there. I finally admitted that I was. I surrendered.

My trip to Tewksbury was rescheduled to December 23, 2012 so I would be missing the holiday season with my family and friends. I was fine with that. I figured it was just another day and I would be all right. I didn't drink or do any drugs when I got out of the McGee Unit and I returned to work for a few weeks until I had to go away to Tewksbury. When I finally arrived back to Tewksbury I had been clean and sober for a few weeks and had a positive attitude upon entering the program. The same guy that gave me the breathalyzer test was there again and he said, "You're back." I smiled.

The whole Tewksbury experience was a life changer for me. I learned a great deal while being there, especially during the holiday season. It was tough, but the people there were amazing, patients and staff included. Some people were there from my hometown so it was nice that I knew a few people. I knew Dalty and I met Adam, who was also from my area. They both were great to have around during my stay. I must say, we played a lot of Spades together!

Speakers came in and there were meetings as well. It was a well-run program that had a tedious schedule, but everything was organized. I referred to this place as a sort of "baby jail" but it wasn't bad at all. The main thing was to follow the rules. I made sure to do that. I never wanted to come back again. Not after my first failed attempt. I didn't want a second.

I met a lot of great people, had a great counselor, and did all of the work that was asked of me. I was honest with my problems. That was my big breakthrough. Being honest with myself and having the courage to share some of my issues. People listened. They didn't judge. Not at Tewksbury. We were all there for the same reason, and I took advantage of that fact. Why not get the best of the experience. Opening up and being honest, whether sharing my experiences, or writing my thoughts down on paper, helped me a great deal.

I made it through the 14-day program and left with a different state of mind. I was focused on recovery. I was focused on staying clean and sober when I returned home. I knew it wasn't going to be easy, but that's what I wanted. I went to a few more AA meetings but soon found out that it wasn't my cup of tea. I decided to take my own route of recovery. I knew I could. I just had to take it one day at a time. I kept it simple. I gained willpower each day I woke up clean and sober. I started growing self-respect. I was feeling better about myself. I was determined to fight this disease. I was determined to beat it one day at a time. One day at a time.

I went back to work for Hillcrest, but before I returned, I had to meet with the Human Resource representative. I had to tell him of my alcoholism and what I was going through. It was tough, but the man felt for me. He was happy that I was taking steps in the right direction towards getting well. I was allowed to go back to work after talking to him. I was back working for Hillcrest. The only difference is that I was now clean and sober. I deserved to be. The kids deserved to see me well, along with the other employees. I was changing. I could feel it. It felt damn good, too. I was happy. I was scared. I was anxious. At least I had feelings now. I was walking in totally different skin. I was walking towards recovery rather than towards insanity.

I refrained from going out and partying with friends. I made sure to stay away from any place that involved alcohol, bars included. I didn't want to put myself in an unsafe situation and set myself up for a possible relapse. Not this early in recovery.
I began watching a lot of movies and documentaries related to alcohol and drugs, and I began to read books and articles as well. I read other people's stories and just tried to learn and understand as much as I could. I counted the days, and each day I woke up, I was grateful that I was still clean and sober. I gained confidence in myself as each day passed and was proud to tell my family and friends the progress I was making. I really had a great support system. My family is the strongest support system I have. They are behind me 100%. A lot of my friends are the same way. It's crazy how much support I get in the community.
I remember the first time I went out to eat with my father and grandfather. It must have been after a month or two of being clean and sober and we went to a benefit dinner. It was the first

time I was around people drinking. I was just staring at the beer bottles as people drank. My father and grandfather decided to drink soda with me. It was really cool. It helped me out. I was able to fight through the temptation. It was my first major encounter with alcohol.

About six months into recovery, I began to go out sometimes with friends as they drank. I knew it wasn't going to be easy, but I decided to try to see if I could fight the temptation. I was able to just drink soda, and although I was on the complete opposite side of the spectrum, I was able to steer away from any encounters with alcohol. My friends began to support me. They wouldn't let me hold a beer in my hand. They wouldn't let me order a beer from the bar. They wouldn't let me and I just went along with it. It worked, and the more I went out, the easier it became. It may sound stupid to some people, but like I said, this is "My Journey," and it's working.

In June, 2013 I experienced how powerful the demon of relapse really is. I was on vacation from work so I had the week off. My parents were on vacation so I had the house to myself. I was sitting in my house all week, alone most of the time, just watching television. I was sitting in a chair on a Friday afternoon and this voice wouldn't get out of my head. "Just drink today, it will be all right. You can do it. Tomorrow you won't drink. Just drink today." The voice kept repeating in my head and I was sitting in an empty house. I finally got off the chair and went outside to my father's truck. I got his keys and was able to find the key to open the closet in the living room. I looked inside and I found a 750 ml bottle of 99 proof schnapps that was unopened. It was one of the bottles that my mother found in my room. I took the bottle out of the closet and sat back down in the chair with it clenched in my hands. "Just open it up and drink some. It will be all right." I was fighting a battle in my own head contemplating whether or not I should drink. I went back and forth in my head for an hour straight as the bottle stared at me, unopened. I then thought about the pros and cons. I was

252 days clean and sober and contemplating to drink. Was there an excuse even to drink? I thought about it for a while and realized how far I have come. I realized that if I drank today then most likely I would drink tomorrow. I asked myself again. Why would I drink today? I figured out that it could quite possibly be out of boredom. When that clicked in my head, I decided to text one of my friends to pick me up just to get me out of the house. I never told him why. I put the bottle back in the closet and locked the door. About a minute later, my brother walks through the door and asks me how I was doing. Seconds later, my parents call me from the beach and ask me how my day was. Just like that. I was grateful that I decided not to drink. That was the closest I've ever been to relapsing. It was a close call, but it's also something I can look back on if the situation ever arises again. I would be able to deal with the aspect of relapse a little better after getting through that episode.

I went through a year of group counseling classes at the Brien Center, and I'll tell you, that place is amazing. The group classes were awesome. I was able to share things to these people that I hadn't told anyone before. I stayed true to myself, shared, and listened. It helped me out a lot during my recovery. I had a great counselor and the people in my group were amazing. I'll never forget them.

I began to take up a few new hobbies during my recovery as well. I got a new mountain bike that I ride during the spring and summer months. We have this bike trail in my hometown called the Ashuwillticook Rail Trail. I usually ride it from my house to the end which is about 26 miles total. It's great to just get out there and see the beauty of nature. It's like a natural high. I also took up hiking, which I grew to love. We have this mountain called Mount Greylock, which is close to where I live and I hike it all the time. It's the tallest mountain in Massachusetts at 3,491 feet. Getting to the peak is well worth the hike. What a beautiful sight! I enjoy being outdoors. Hiking and biking suit me well. I am able to exercise and enjoy the true beauty of the world around me. It's a vital guideline to my recovery.

Towards the end of October, 2013 I was 11 months clean and sober and an opportunity for a new job arose. I interviewed for a paraprofessional job at Charles H. McCann Technical High School. I would be specifically working with special needs students. The next day, I received a phone call and accepted the job at the high school. I told my employer at Hillcrest that I would work two final weeks with them. Saying goodbye to my students was one of the hardest things I ever had to do. I was sad to say goodbye to the kids and my fellow employees. I would miss them all. I mean that from the bottom of my heart. Hillcrest changed my life. But it was time to move on with my life, and I took the opportunity to make more money and work closer to home.

I began working for McCann Technical High School during the start of the school year in September, 2013. So far things are going great. I plan on going back to college to receive my master's degree (looking towards a master's of special education). I want to teach the youth. I enjoy working with kids, especially those who need the extra help. Throughout my life, I always needed extra help. I was just afraid to ask. I relied on drugs and alcohol for the answers. It seemed as if I was always learning the hard way.

It turned out that the more mistakes I made, the easier it became to turn off the lights on society. I don't want anyone to have to learn the way I did. I was fortunate. It's a blessing. I am grateful for each and every new day that arises. I am grateful that I found that moment of clarity. I am grateful that I found the strength to keep fighting. I am grateful for the people around me. I am grateful to live another day, freed from the realms of drugs and alcohol. At the beginning of this story, I mentioned that I wanted to help, reach out, and inspire others. I hope I did. I have been clean and sober since November 25,

2012. I still walk around this Earth with skin and bones, but I carry a few ounces of courage that fatten me up.

Made in the USA
Charleston, SC
14 March 2014